Better Homes and Gardens®

Gardening Made Easy

Meredith® Consumer Marketing

Better Homes and Gardens® GARDENING MADE EASY
Editor: Karen Weir-Jimerson
Designers: Sundie Ruppert, Brad Ruppert
Art Director: Tim Alexander
Technical Editor: Denny Schrock
Copy Editor: Sarah Gold
Proofreaders: Ira Lacher, Kelly Roberson
Indexer: Ellen Sherron
Fact Checker: Diana Dickinson

Better Homes and Gardens® Magazine
Editor in Chief: Gayle Goodson Butler
Editor in Chief, Gardening: Doug Jimerson
Executive Editor: Kitty Morgan
Managing Editor: Lamont D. Olson
Art Director: Michael D. Belknap

Meredith Publishing Group
President: Jack Griffin
Executive Vice President: Doug Olson
Vice President, Manufacturing: Bruce Heston
Vice President, Consumer Marketing: David Ball
Director, Consumer Product Marketing: Kathi Prien
Director, Production: Douglas M. Johnston
Business Manager: Todd Voss

Meredith Corporation
Chairman of the Board: William T. Kerr
President and Chief Executive Officer: Stephen M. Lacy
In Memoriam: E.T. Meredith III (1933-2003)

Contributing Photographers
Adam Albright, King Au, Quentin Bacon, Marty Baldwin, André Baranowski, Alison Barnes, Edmund Barr, Gordon Beall, Matthew Benson, Laurie Black, Rob Cardillo, Walter Chandoha, Kim Cornelison, Jack Coyier, Stephen Cridland, R. Todd Davis, Erica George Dines, Jason Donnelly, Andrew Drake, Colleen Duffley, Clint Farlinger, Richard Felber, Derek Fell, Emily Followill, John Reed Forsman, Carol Freeman, Ed Gohlich, David Goldberg, John Granen, Bob Greenspan, Mick Hales, Justin Hancock, Amy Haskell, Chipper R. Hatter, Doug Hetherington, Richard Hirneisen, Bill Holt, William N. Hopkins, Roy Inman, Jon Jensen, Michael Jensen, Graham Jimerson, Dency Kane, Mark Kane, Lynn Karlin, Keller & Keller, Kritsada, Peter Krumhardt, Scott Little, Janet Loughrey, Sherry Lubic, Andy Lyons, Allan Mandell, Barbara Martin, Bryan E. McCay, David McDonald, Steven McDonald, Jeff McNamara, Tom McWilliam, Janet Mesic-Mackie, Emily Minton-Redfield, Blaine Moats, Shawn Nielsen, John Noltner, Helen Norman, Michael Partenio, Jerry Pavia, Celia Pearson, Dan Piassick, Eric Roth, Greg Ryan, Cameron Sadeghpour, Greg Scheidemann, Randall Schieber, Dean Schoeppner, Denny Schrock, Douglas Smith, David Speer, Julie Sprott, Bob Stefko, Bill Stites, Marilyn Stouffer, Rick Taylor, Andreas Trauttmansdorff, Jane Booth Vollers, Tony Walsh, Richard Warren, Judith Watts, Virginia Weller, Jay Wilde

Contributing Color Garden Illustrator
Mavis Torke

Contributing Cover Photographer
Jay Wilde

Printed in the United States of America.
ISBN: 978-0-696-24358-5

All of us at Meredith Consumer Marketing are dedicated to providing you with information and ideas to enhance your home and garden. We welcome your comments and suggestions. Write to us at:
Meredith Consumer Marketing
1716 Locust Street
Des Moines, IA 50309-3023

Note to the readers: Due to differing conditions, tools and individual skills, Meredith Corporation assumes no responsibility for any damages, injuries suffered or losses incurred as a result of following the information published in this book. Before beginning any project, review the instructions carefully, and if any doubts or questions remain, consult local experts or authorities. Because codes and regulations vary greatly, you always should check with authorities to ensure that your project complies with all applicable local codes and regulations. Always read and observe all of the safety precautions provided by manufacturers of any tools, equipment or supplies, and follow all accepted safety procedures.

Pictured on the front cover: Plant a butterfly garden with these favorites: Zinnia ‘Profusion White,’ Zinnia ‘Zahara White,’ Petunia ‘Blue Wave,’ Pentas ‘Butterfly Red,’ Celosia ‘Smart Look Red,’ Buddleja ‘Adonis Blue,’ Salvia ‘Evolution,’ Lantana ‘Radiation,’ Canna ‘Black Night,’ *Canna indica*, Calamagrostis.

Pictured on the back cover: Sunflower, Columbine

contents

84 **CHAPTER FOUR**

easy garden plans

Choose the type of garden that's best for your yard. Plans, plant lists, flower profiles and step-by-step instructions help you create the garden of your dreams.

194 **CHAPTER FIVE**

picking the right plants

Grow flowers and foliage everywhere in your yard! It's easy when you know what plants need for success.

262 **CHAPTER SIX**

tools and essentials

From soil to fertilizer to which pruner works best in the garden—gear up for gardening.

INTRODUCTION

Gardening will change your life. If you think that's a dramatic statement, then consider this: Gardening is all about connecting to and creating things that are beautiful and real such as fabulous flowers, fresh food, inspiring color combinations, fragrance and wildlife. Gardening gets you out into the world, moving and stretching and creating. Tending a garden is the perfect antidote to a stressful life—because you get to impose order over a small part of the world.

Dig in, but be realistic. Like every new hobby, it's easy to get totally enchanted—then overwhelmed. Start small and expand your garden gradually and you'll be pleased with the results. Consider your lifestyle as you build your garden. Ask yourself how much of your day or week you can care for your garden. Also factor in how much inspiration, flowers or fresh herbs you can produce in your life. This will help you decide what kind and size of garden you should plant and how much time you want to spend there.

This book presents the essential elements of gardening. Like many other important life skills, gardening is a hobby that you learn more about the more you do it. You discover small but miraculous things in your own backyard: the nuances of flower color as the light changes, the joy of seeing a bud unfurl into a bloom, the pleasure of picking a tomato and eating it, still warmed by the sun. Your garden teaches you about growth, color, beauty, life and renewal.

Choosing plants is a bit like making new friends. You hang around those you like (and who like you). And then you discover new friends, and they become part of your circle. Gardening is about creating relationships. Finding two flowers you think look beautiful together is the first step in understanding the complexity and choreography of a good garden plan.

This book presents the best of the spirit of gardening. It teaches you about color and texture. It shows you how to do basic gardening acts such as planting a rose or sowing lettuce seeds. And it offers beautiful and well-designed garden plans, with plant lists so you can create your garden exactly the way you see it in the photo. You'll also find beautiful plant combinations that may set you thinking about dreaming up your own garden designs. You'll find very quickly that gardening grows more than plants—it grows creativity.

And that's what gardening is all about—growing, loving and tending the little piece of earth that you call home. Happy gardening!

Chapter One

THE BENEFITS OF GARDENING

When you plant a garden, you nurture more than plants. You also cultivate knowledge, grow your own creativity and learn to respect the connection between you and the Earth.

"I love picking lettuce from my garden and serving it just minutes later. That's fresh!" —Annie

Plant a Garden!

Whether you tuck flowers into a window box, plant a rosebush next to your front door or line out vegetables in a sunny spot in your backyard, gardening produces beautiful results.

No one is born knowing how to garden. Perhaps your grandmother or grandfather had a garden. Or your mother or father did. But many of us didn't grow up with a gardening mentor. The good news is that it's never too late to start gardening. Because there is no age—no matter how young or old you are—that gardening *isn't* a satisfying hobby.

Gardening is a lifetime hobby too. It's an activity that keeps teaching you new things. Every day that you garden you grow your knowledge about how to plant, care for, harvest and enjoy what you have sown. Thomas Jefferson, who created magnificent gardens at his home, Monticello, said, "Though an old man, I am but a young gardener."

Your garden knowledge grows with every act of gardening you perform. Gardening is cumulative and transferable. Once you know how to plant a seedling, you also know how to plant a perennial or an annual. So the simple act of planting, say, a pot of marigolds also prepares you to plant your first vegetable garden or rose garden.

Of course each plant has its own schedule, its own way of growing and specific needs. For example, some plants like sun. Others shrivel up from too much sun. But once you have a garden, or a container filled with flowers, or a tomato plant that bears its first fruit, you start to see the needs of your plants and the logic of gardening.

You can harvest lettuce leaves just weeks after your seeds germinate. Watching the tiny green sprouts push up and out of the soil is nothing less than miraculous.

sow a seed ...

The famous English garden designer Gertrude Jekyll once said, "The love of gardening is a seed once sown that never dies." And as you grow as a gardener you will understand and feel the benefits. Gardening is great if you want to:

Cultivate your creativity. Your yard is an extension of your home. And like decorating your home, gardening is a creative activity. It's a way to express yourself and your loves. How does your creativity grow? Some of us love the artfulness of raising a garden for salad, or planting a rose for its beautiful fresh-cut flowers. Creating a garden that matches your home style—for example, a traditional garden or a cottage garden—gives you another way to replicate the styles that appeal to you. And some of us just love to revel in the pure exuberant color that a garden brings to a yard.

Reduce your stress levels. The world we live in is fast-paced—we're told to expect instant gratification. All the rushing and high expectations lead to stress. And gardening appears on nearly every "stress buster" list. That's because the activities of gardening—planting, weeding, picking flowers—involve moving, being outdoors and creating beauty. Adages like "stop and smell the roses" were coined for a reason—because gardening reduces stress.

Increase life satisfaction. Gardening can help you feel that you've accomplished something big, something important, something of value. And that's a satisfying feeling. Plant a seed, and it grows into a flowering plant that brings beauty to your yard. Or harvest vegetables and serve your family a meal that you've grown yourself.

Get moving. Cancel your gym membership because gardening can be your new workout. An hour of gardening burns up approximately 250 calories. Hoeing weeds stretches back muscles. Trimming hedges works your upper arms and chest. And digging planting beds tones arms and legs.

Give yourself flowers. It's no surprise to anyone who has gotten flowers for Valentine's Day or another special occasion how much the sight and scent of a bouquet lifts your spirits. So just imagine how thankful you'll feel when you step outside into your garden every day. Give yourself a bouquet once a week. And share the happiness with friends and family. Everyone loves fresh flowers on the kitchen table.

Enjoy safe and nutritious food. If you grow your garden organically, you can enjoy fruits and vegetables that are free of pesticides and other unsafe ingredients that can end up in processed food. If you grow nutritious food you will be more likely to eat it—and really enjoy the fruits of your labors.

Increase your home's value. Many real estate studies have shown that curb appeal improves the value of your home. Your landscaping, gardens and colorful flowers all enhance your home's look—hence its value. Plants can even cover up unattractive parts of your home such as the concrete block foundation or a chain-link fence.

Protect the environment. There are so many ways gardening helps you improve your relationship with the earth. Gardening reaffirms your partnership with nature. Your garden gives you the opportunity to sample foods and enjoy flowers that are native to your area. You grow plants that recycle carbon dioxide and create oxygen, which we need to breathe. Trees shade your home, allowing you to use less energy for heating and cooling.

Save money. Whether you grow a small pot of basil to season summer salads and pasta dishes (have you checked out the grocery store prices for herbs?) or you put in rows of tomatoes, you can save money by growing your own vegetables, fruits, herbs and flowers.

Create your own haven. When you cultivate a beautiful garden you're carving out a place you can call your own. Think of your garden as an outdoor room and deck it out to fit your needs. A small bistro table and chairs surrounded by fragrant roses gives you a serene spot to start the day with a cup of coffee and the sound of birds. A vine-covered pergola sheltering a dining table and chairs gives you ample alfresco space to entertain friends and family. And a bench beside a gurgling water garden provides the perfect setting to relax after a day at work.

Chapter Two

WHAT'S YOUR GARDEN STYLE?

Create a garden plan that fits your yard—and your personality—and you'll be truly happy with the result

Define Your Garden Style

What is the state of your yard? It might be a blank slate ready for a bold new vision. Maybe you installed a landscaping plan several years ago, but now your needs or style have changed. Or you may have inherited a landscape that just isn't you. Whatever type of space you have, you can make it yours with your own style.

What makes you happy? If you met with a garden designer, he or she would ask you what kind of garden makes you happy. Do you like flowers? Do you love the color blue? Do you want a low-maintenance garden? Do you yearn to hear the trickle of flowing water as you sip a cup of tea? The answers to these questions will help you define your style and get you closer to creating your dream garden.

Visualize your garden. Start by collecting photos from magazines or bookmark books to help you see what you like best about a specific type of garden. For example, if you select a lot of photos with roses, you know you need to add roses to your plant list. If you clip out photos of flower-filled gardens in swaths of pastels, you'll get an idea of what type of color scheme most appeals to you. You may be drawn to photos of brick paths edged with tightly clipped hedges. Envisioning these individual elements will also help you design the garden that will make you happy.

Consider color. Planting a flower garden allows you to indulge yourself by surrounding your home with blooms in your favorite color. You can paint your landscape with soft pastels or rev it up with bright, bold colors. If you want a subtle and sophisticated look, try a garden with all-white flowers. You also can choose plants that offer color in every season; for example, some shrubs feature red or yellow stems that look great all winter.

Design with your heart. In addition to "seeing" what your garden will look like by collecting photos of elements you find attractive, it's important to design a garden around the lifestyle you want. Picture yourself in your garden, then write the scenario down in a notebook. Use these notes to help you determine the elements you should have in your garden. "I want to eat outdoors" means you need a dining area. "I'd like to have my morning coffee while feeding koi in my water garden" means you need a seating area next to a water garden. "I want to smell fragrant flowers as I walk through my garden" means you need a pathway lined with scented blooms. This type of experiential "wish list" will help you design the kind of garden you want.

Plant with practicality. You need to assess your garden's location and plan and plant with practicality. For example, if your backyard is fully shaded, you can have a lovely shade garden. But you will not be able to grow tomatoes because they need full sun. If you want a cactus garden but live in a cold climate, you may have to make some compromises and plant in containers. If you travel every other week for work, you may not want a garden that requires lots of care. Take into consideration your yard as well as your time and choose a garden that will flourish within the constraints of both.

Be authentic or mix and match. Each style—formal, cottage, contemporary, Asian—has specific characteristics that define it. Types of plans, plants, water features, structures and materials are the elements you can use to replicate a specific look. For some gardeners, staying within guidelines of specific style is what expresses beauty to them. It's kind of like following a recipe. For others, mixing and matching style elements expresses best what they want their gardens to be. Gardening, like home décor or the way you wear your hair, is all a matter of personal expression.

"On a recent trip to England I toured several formal gardens. How I can bring that style home—on a smaller scale?" —Melissa

The Classicist: Formal Style

Formal gardens appeal to gardeners for a variety of reasons. If your home is built in a traditional architectural style, you may want a garden that reflects its exterior details. For example, if your house has a red brick façade with white trim, you may find that brick walkways and a pair of white urns are a beautiful way to continue the style of your house throughout your garden. Or you may enjoy the simplicity of a formal garden because it exhibits a strong sense of organization: the symmetry of geometric flowerbeds, the repetition of massed plantings and the order of linear pathways.

You also may be drawn to a formal garden because you enjoy the sense of history and grandeur. Formal gardens have been a feature of stately homes in England since the time of Shakespeare. It is the style of most estate gardens in France and Italy as well—each culture adding its particular design spin. Historically the design of formal gardens expressed the humanistic philosophy that man was the center of the universe. Examples of this formal style can be seen at the gardens of the Château of Versailles in France, where grand scale and precise geometry were employed to glorify the power of the 17th-century Sun King, Louis XIV.

In a formal garden, paths are laid out along a main axis, which often leads from the portals of the house (the front door, the back door, an arbor or archway) to a distant focal point such as a bench, an urn or a piece of sculpture. By continuing the geometry of the house outdoors, a formal layout creates a transition to a wild or informal landscape at the property's edge.

This symmetrical parterre garden features the requisite low boxwood hedges with two 'Tardiva' hydrangea standards planted in each rectangular bed to add height and structure.

FORMAL STYLE: ELEMENTS

The Design

A formal garden *(right)* always has a focal point. A piece of sculpture, an architectural feature or a water source (a pond studded with water lilies, a fountain or a birdbath) all draw the eye to the center of the garden. Surrounding the focal point are flowerbeds arranged in parallel rectangles, squares or circles. The beds are usually edged with low, clipped hedges (boxwood is a common choice) and filled with masses of annuals or perennials that provide dramatic but controlled color displays. Planting beds are often separated by narrow pathways. The paths in a formal garden can be made of a variety of materials: brick, pea gravel and crushed seashells. In short, a formal garden is the sum of many elements, all of which are easy even for novice gardeners to emulate.

Formal Plants

There are several iconic formal garden plants, but nothing says "formal garden" more than boxwood (*Buxus sempervirens*). Used for topiary, hedges and parterres, this leafy green shrub often serves as the dominant structural plant in formal gardens. Boxwood can be used in so many ways in a formal garden in part because of its many types; it is available in prostrate, globe, half-erect, weeping, columnar and pyramidal forms. Boxwood also grows to a wide range of sizes and can be sculpted to any shape—into square or rounded hedges or clipped, à la Edward Scissorhands, into topiary animals or geometric shapes. Other must-have plants in a formal garden include roses and herbs such as lavender and rosemary. Standards—tree forms—of roses, hydrangeas and other plants also are frequently found in formal gardens. But any plant can take on a sense of formality when planted *en masse* inside a hedged bed. And the symmetrical placement of a plant—for example, a shrub planted on either side of a walkway—adds a formal feel, as does a line of pairs of trees (called an allée). Individual plants, such as evergreens that exhibit a uniform appearance naturally, also are frequent additions to a formal garden.

HEDGE YOUR BEDS

Clipped hedges are the "bones" of a formal garden. Evergreen hedges look good through four seasons.

Yew
Boxwood
Mountain Laurel
Myrtle
Holly
Arborvitae

Hardscaping

Brick is a classic formal garden material used both for paths and walls. The rectangular shape of each brick echoes the geometric design throughout the garden. Wooden lattice trellises and archways also are classic structures in a formal garden. A traditional element from the 18th century is a folly, a small building that actually is more decorative than functional. Today, traditional gardeners may use a potting shed as a folly replacement.

Water Features

Water adds reflective beauty and gentle sound to the formal garden. Examples of formal water features include fountains, reflecting ponds, and water gardens that feature classic aqua plantings such as lotuses or water lilies. Fountains set in shallow geometrical basins mimic the geometry of the bed design. Inground water features are generally geometric in shape—circular, square or rectangular. Sculptures that incorporate a fountain are ways to include both water and statuary in a formal garden scheme.

Accessories

Columns and benches (natural teak or painted) are iconic accessories in a formal garden. Used as focal points for the entire garden or just as a centerpiece in a bed, pedestals, pillars, sculptures, statuary and urns recall the architecture of ancient Greece, ancient Rome and more recent classical revivals. Potted plants may be topiaries clipped into globes or swirls. *At right,* Sir Edwin Lutyens' famous oak bench inspired this now classic icon of the formal garden.

"I want a lush and flower-filled garden. And I don't mind things looking a little wild." —Monica

The Romantic: Cottage Style

Cottage gardens express a joy and passion for color, texture and nature. They started as humble but vibrant spaces that grew within fenced-in plots kept by rural cottagers who loved flowers for their fragrant beauty, used herbs for their medicinal properties and grew fruits and vegetables to feed their families. Today's cottage gardens retain that feel, and cottage style has become synonymous with a simpler and slower time.

Flowers are the main event in the cottage garden, and "the more the merrier" rule applies here. Plants of different heights, colors and textures are all welcome. But old-fashioned flowers play a big role: fragrant cabbage roses, patrician hollyhocks and delphiniums, and the cheery open faces of sunflowers, bachelor's buttons, daisies and cosmos all create a delirious display of color and bloom.

Although cottage gardens grow from distinct plans and may contain elements of a formal garden, there is more of a sense of fun, humor and whimsy. A cottage garden focal point may be a mass of morning glories growing on an old, rusted farm gate. A collection of old olive oil cans may find new life as planters. A cottage garden is all about reusing, refashioning and recycling bits of the past into pieces of beauty and art.

Some people refer to a cottage garden as a country garden partly because you'll likely find aspects of country and agricultural life there—old tractor parts, windmills, galvanized tanks used as water gardens. And truly these gardens are cousins, because an agrarian past links them to the land.

A cottage garden is at home in the city—or a suburban neighborhood—as well as in the country because "cottage" is a sense of style. For some a cottage garden is too disorderly and messy. But for cottage garden fans, that sense of wild growth and disorder is exactly what makes their gardens into havens. Once established, a cottage garden is fairly low-maintenance and needs very little weeding, as even the most invasive pest can't find a roothold in the thick mass of plants.

Cottage gardeners roll out the welcome mat for nature. Many gardens feature birdhouses, feeders and baths as focal points. And the quintessential cottage garden barrier—the picket fence—offers a beautiful backdrop for campanula and roses.

COTTAGE STYLE: ELEMENTS

The Design

A mass of blooms, a rush of color and the sweet fragrance of flowers make a cottage garden seem like the antithesis of the control and order of a formal garden. Yet cottage gardens have specific design elements too. If a cottage garden is large, it will have paths that lead to the different areas. If it is small, it may just feature simple flat stepping stones. Since cottage gardens often include kitchen gardens—including herb beds—paths are necessary for movement throughout the garden. Cottage garden pathways are usually made of natural and rustic materials such as stones, shredded bark mulch, pine needle mulch or pea gravel. Paths may have no edgings, or field or river stones of varying sizes and colors may be placed to create a barrier between beds and paths. Frequently, cottage gardens use potting sheds as anchors (sort of a throwback to the tiny cottages from which this style was derived), which also serves as a spot to sit and enjoy the view.

Cottage Garden Plants

Cottage gardens are all about big color. Early spring brings a lush display of gorgeous blooming bulbs, from swaying red tulips to sunny daffodils. Perennials that include long-blooming daylilies and lily bulbs are cottage garden standards. Big, bold flowering shrubs, such as Chinese snowball (*Viburnum macrocephalum*) and blue and pink hydrangea (*Hydrangea macrophylla*), add structure as well as vase-loads of flowers all summer. Old-fashioned heirloom annual vines, morning glory, for example (try the sky-blue 'Heavenly Blue' and purple-striped 'Grandpa Ott's'), cypress vine and black-eyed Susan vine, all are great choices for a cottage garden. Grow them on a trellis, over an arbor or intertwined through the pickets of a fence.

COTTAGE GARDEN FLOWERS
Favorite cottage garden flowers have common traits. They are great cut flowers and may bear wonderful fragrance—or both. Here's a list of the top 10 cottage perennials:
Columbine
Lavender
Lily of the Valley
Poppy
Bleeding Heart
Daisy
Pinks
Peony
Delphinium
Iris

Hardscaping

Arbors are a must-have item for a cottage garden. As an inviting entryway or a garden focal point, an arbor creates a pleasing structure that also is a great place to grow plants. Roses are a favorite cottage garden flower, especially the old-fashioned ones that are big and petal-packed. Climbing roses (*above*) offer gorgeous blooms, a lovely scent and ruby-red or orange rose hips in the fall. Because cottage gardens were originally the fenced-in areas around small cottages, fencing is a standard element. White pickets create a lovely backdrop for blooming flowers. Wattle, a woven twig fencing popular in England, also is an option. Stone walls, either dry-stacked or mortared, create a natural-looking barrier.

Water Features

All gardens benefit from the soothing sound of water, and cottage gardens are no exception. Rustic and simple water sources include a bucket fountain (*above*) or water bubbling up through an old millstone. Cottage gardens frequently feature inground or container water gardens that offer cool sips to birds and butterflies. Other water features may include rustic stone troughs and decorative birdbaths.

Accessories

Cottage gardens emphasize nature and wildlife, so many accessories feature these themes. Birdhouses (*right*) and feeders offer housing and food to encourage more species to visit the garden. Bee skeps (*above*) are frequently used as centerpieces in herb beds, although they are ornamental and rarely attract bees. Cottage gardens have no rules on what fits. Found or repurposed objects often are used as ornaments. For example, a trio of long-handled tools can be made into a flower tepee. A barn cupola can become a focal point when placed in the center of a garden. If you find beauty in a rustic piece of statuary, an old garden sign or old piece of farm equipment, add it to your cottage garden.

"I like a clean and contemporary look and modern furniture. How can I do that with a garden?" —Carina

The Modernist: Contemporary Style

A contemporary garden incorporates structure, art and texture in a simple but dramatic way. As with contemporary architecture and furniture design, form follows function. So contemporary gardens are spare but usable. Perhaps the best thing about a contemporary landscape is that it incorporates high style but is usually quite low-maintenance.

Most contemporary garden design is inspired by the design of the home—modern homes beget contemporary gardens. However, you don't have to own a home built with concrete, chrome and glass to plant a contemporary garden. Those clean, minimalist design tenets apply to the gardens of a bungalow, saltbox or farmhouse style of home.

Contemporary gardens rely on plants for their structural and textural attributes more than for their ability to bloom in bright colors. So many contemporary gardens have a very "green" look to them. Blooming plants can be used but are usually accents, not the main event. Plants are selected for their individual looks—either when used alone or for the pattern they create when combined in multiples. For example, ornamental grasses are often featured in contemporary garden design because they have such consistent and predictable growth habits. Large, feathery grasses, such as leatherleaf sedge, look statuesque standing alone. But when planted in multiples in a geometric grid, they take on an entirely different presentation. Cacti—there are hundreds of choices—give contemporary gardeners a palette of textures filled with twists, turns, spikes and folds. If you live in a cold climate, plant these tender beauties in containers and bring them indoors to overwinter.

Burro's tail, which emulates cascading streams of water, spills over the side of a long planter. Ornamental grasses create a spray of monochromatic foliage.

The Design

Contemporary gardens are uncluttered yet inviting, spare yet vibrant. Many gardens are built with the house or walls as a backdrop to the garden. Gardens can be installed in the ground, or in containers or planters. Repetition of plants and design motifs creates a sense of continuity. Planting schemes can include snuggling plants close together to create a continuous line of foliage, or positioning plants with lots of air and space around them so they can be viewed as individual elements.

Hardscaping

Planting beds are geometrically angular or circular and can range in size, depending on the space available. Some beds can be quite large—if space allows—but sparsely planted. Paving materials are natural, taking advantage of what Mother Nature has to offer in terms of texture and color, and include slate, large and small stones and gravel. Manmade materials also are used in creative ways. Metal, glass and tile add color or reflect light. Even mulch can take on a modern look, with slate or colored stone serving as a ground covering.

TEXTURAL PLANTS
Contemporary gardens call for plants that are, on their own, visually interesting but not necessarily colorful. Here is a list of plants that have textural talent:
Lamb's Ears
Yucca
Sedum
Barrel Cactus
Sago Palm
Euphorbia
Hen and Chickens
Equisetum
Ornamental Grasses
Kalanchoe

Contemporary Garden Plants

Succulents and cacti are favorite contemporary garden plants because they feature so many textural possibilities. Tall, spiky foliage plants, such as century plant (*Agave*), sago palm (*Cycas revoluta*) and ornamental grasses (*Miscanthus, Carex*), create a sense of architecture. Succulent plants offer textural lushness. Try hen and chickens (*Sempervivum tectorum*) and sedums such as burro's tail (*Sedum morganianum*).

Water Features

Contemporary garden water features use manmade materials, or natural materials used in a modern way. Narrow water strips surrounded by cut stone can be filled with architectural water plants that include frilly topped papyrus (*Cyperus*) or bamboo look-alike horsetail (*Equisetum*). Rusted iron, stainless and galvanized steel or subdued-hued ceramic are used to create bubbling fountains or vessels to hold water gardens.

Accessories

Contemporary gardens call for modern furnishings, from angular or curvy chaise lounges to sit-back-in-comfort sling-back chairs. Dining and side tables may be constructed from wood or metal and topped with glass or natural stone slabs. Art—especially abstract, freeform sculptures—is a common focal point in a modern garden. Containers and planters follow basic geometric design. Terra-cotta is a classic choice, as are pots made from metal, stone or wood.

"I'm a little country, a little Zen and I like lots of flowers—that's my garden style." —Elsie

The Individualist: Personal Style

How do you create your own personal garden? Just tap into your passion and plant it your way. Forget about following an established garden style—create your own! After all it's your garden, so surround yourself with the flowers, furnishings and accessories that make you happy. Going with your personal style, sometimes called eclectic, gives you permission to do as you like—to break all the rules. You can include features of formal, country, kitchen and Asian gardens all in the same space.

Personal gardens are born out of passion. Do you love the color pink? Then decorate your garden in pink plus—pink flowers, pink lounge chairs, pink garden ornaments. Or maybe you are a collector and have objects that can establish a theme: watering cans, blue glass bottles, bowling balls; all can find a place in your garden. Perhaps you are enamored with a specific animal or insect such as dogs, cats, chickens, cows, frogs or butterflies. From statuary to topiary you can pay homage to your favorite creatures in your garden.

A personal garden also can follow a plant-inspired theme. Some gardeners are simply obsessed with one type of plant, so they have a garden filled exclusively with, say, hostas. Or roses. Or cacti. And some gardeners erase the common conceptions of what defines a garden and mix food crops into their flowerbeds. After all, what's so odd about finding salad greens next to annual flowers, or strawberries as edging plants along a pathway?

A piece of art or statuary may be the inspiration for a personal garden. Or a found-object focal point, such as a repurposed barn cupola, may be the starting point. Personal gardens are part plant and part whimsy—for example, a "garden bed" planted within an old bed frame, complete with headboard.

And don't feel afraid to mix and match styles. A formal accessory, such as an urn or spiraling topiary evergreen, can look right at home in a cottage garden. It's your style and your decision about what you include.

Mix it up! So what if you don't live in the tropics? You still can grow bananas right in the center of your garden—surrounded by a formal boxwood bed with a country-inspired iron rooster in front.

personal style: elements

The Design

A personal garden should, above all, be a comfortable placc. Soft seating, surrounding lush greenery and colorful flowers and the soothing sound of moving water create a private getaway. Furnish your personal garden with eclectic outdoor décor and plantings—mix old furniture with fabrics in contemporary patterns and intermingle tropical plants with perennials. It's all about the fusion of the things you like.

TOP GARDEN COLLECTIBLES

Use objects you've collected to infuse your personality into the garden. Here are some ideas:

STATUARY THEMES
Fairies
Gnomes
Cats
Dogs
Chickens
Toads

GARDEN ORNAMENTS
Bee Skeps
Cloches
Old Gardening Tools
Garden Gates
Gazing Balls

Personal Garden Plants

Group plants with collectibles (such as old birdcages) to make little vignettes in your garden. Make planters out of discarded olive oil or gallon-size tomato cans. (Leave the labels on!) Or you can choose a plant theme that fits your interest: an all-heirloom garden; an alphabet garden with plantings that run the gamut from A to Z; or a garden planted with flowers that attract and feed butterflies and plants their larvae need to survive.

Water Features

Personal garden style gives you the freedom to have some fun. Add water to your garden in nontraditional ways. You can plumb nearly anything to create a fountain. Pair up an old teapot with a water pump to make a tabletop fountain. Or simply take a large ceramic bowl and fill it with water lettuce to create a lush tabletop water garden.

Accessories

Humor is a good place to start. Head planters sprouting green thoughts, a bottle tree festooned with blue bottles—whatever tickles your fancy is a good addition to your garden. Your collection of watering cans or garden gnomes—display them all with pride. Multiples make a personal statement. Or add signs with inspirational phrases such as "Believe," Stop and Smell the Roses" and "It's Thyme to Garden" to express yourself.

"I want to taste food that was picked five minutes ago. Plus, I save money when I grow my own herbs." —Helen

The Cook: Kitchen Style

A kitchen garden is one of the oldest types of garden. Called potager gardens in Europe, they were essential parts of wealthy estates and provided food for the household and staff. On a smaller scale, kitchen gardens sprang up in sunny strips alongside cottages and frontier homes; they were the grocery stores of their day. Feeding a family from the garden took some planning and many crops, so kitchen gardens were designed with the goal of growing as many different types of foods as possible.

Modern kitchen gardening has a somewhat different appeal. You may not be able to feed your family exclusively from your garden. But you can grow heirloom and specialty vegetables, fruits and herbs—varieties you just can't find in the grocery store. And you'll enjoy the freshest produce ever, literally minutes from the garden to the plate. Plus, if organic food is your preference, you can raise everything without pesticides and herbicides so you'll know you are eating produce that is chemical-free.

Kitchen gardens can simply be plots of land with row crops of your favorite vegetables. Or you can design a beautiful and hardworking kitchen garden using raised beds. Raised-bed gardening solves the problem of poor soil—you add your own. And because the bed sits on the ground, you don't have to worry about clay or rocky soils. This type of bed allows closer spacing of vegetables because you don't need to walk between rows. The bed's height keeps out encroaching weeds and grass, so weeding is minimized.

Raised beds can be made any size, and something as small as a 4×4-foot garden can produce a lot of food. Construct beds of naturally rot-resistant woods such as redwood, cedar and cypress. Or try synthetic options that include composite decking materials (made from a mixture of recycled plastic and wood byproducts), stone and landscape timbers.

A vegetable garden can be beautiful from spring to fall when you add flowering annuals and perennials to the mix.

KITCHEN GARDEN STYLE: ELEMENTS

The Design

Kitchen gardens come in all sizes, and their design is based on the goal of producing the most food in the most efficient manner. But that doesn't mean kitchen gardens also aren't beautiful. Many use raised beds to facilitate planting, growth and harvest, and these geometrically shaped beds make a kitchen garden look organized and orderly. At the center of many kitchen gardens is an herb garden, frequently with an interesting focal point sculpture or ornament. Of course what you plant will help dictate how your garden is organized and designed. For example, if you want to grow grapes, you need a support structure such as a pergola or a fence. There may be room in your kitchen garden for fruit trees. Use dwarf varieties or train them to grow against a wall (espalier). Or you can set them in an allée (a parallel successive planting flanking a path) leading to the entrance of the kitchen garden.

Kitchen Garden Plants

What do you like to eat? The answer is what you should plant in your garden. By planning successive crops—both cool- and warm-weather vegetables—you can harvest vegetables and herbs continuously throughout the spring, summer and fall. In the early spring grow lettuce, greens (such as mesclun mix, mustard and arugula), peas, radishes, carrots and broccoli. After you've harvested your cool-weather crops, plant hot-weather favorites such as tomatoes, peppers, eggplant and herbs. Train tomato plants into towers or cages to keep them vertical. In fall you can harvest potatoes, cabbages and kale. And even if you have limited space, you can enjoy fruits such as apples and pears. Some dwarf varieties can be grown in containers on your patio.

SAVE MONEY!

Packs of seeds cost a couple of dollars. Sow them directly into the ground to save time. (No transplanting seedlings.) Here are easy-start options:

- Peas
- Beans
- Squash
- Lettuce
- Mesclun Mix
- Beets
- Kale
- Broccoli
- Radishes
- Carrots

VEGGIE CLASSICS

CARROTS An early season crop, carrots can be harvested in 65 days.

LEEKS This member of the onion family takes 110 days to reach maturity.

TOMATOES From large heirlooms to tiny cherry tomatoes—just take your pick.

CABBAGE Two crops of cabbage are possible, in spring and autumn.

Herb Garden

Most kitchen gardens feature a separate herb garden, which is a smart way to raise the most expensive type of produce. Generally an herb garden is a square or round bed filled with tender herbs, such as basil, cilantro and rosemary, and perennial herbs, such as chives, thyme, oregano and mint. Herbs offer healthy ways to enhance the flavor of food without adding lots of calories.

Hardscaping

Kitchen gardening is all about the efficient use of space. Crops are packed in shoulder to shoulder to enable you to get the best yields. Some vegetables, such as tomatoes, need lots of space to grow. Adding towers, cages or other supports keeps them growing up and not over your other vegetables. A towers can be a sturdy, defined structure that adds a formal feel to the garden (*above*). Or it can be rustic, such as a tepee fashioned from three twigs to support an early crop of snap peas.

Accessories

Kitchen gardens may feature utilitarian but beautiful accessories. For example, the terra-cotta plant blanchers *at right* set over the top of a growing plant to protect it from the light. Blanching pots keep plants that include rhubarb, asparagus and celery from turning green; the vegetables underneath stay white. Other kitchen garden accessories include bee skeps and sundials, both traditional centerpieces for herb gardens. And garden cloches—glass, bell-shaped coverings (*above*) that protect plants from temperature extremes—also are beautiful garden ornaments.

"I'm really into the texture of plants. I love the colors and shapes of cacti and succulents." —Theresa

The Specialist: Theme Gardens

There are many different styles of gardens that don't fit into the formal, cottage, contemporary, kitchen garden and personal garden categories. They reflect an interest in a specific kind of garden that may be influenced by a historical, geographical or situational motif.

Gardens that incorporate natural elements include ***Asian gardens.*** Naturalistic and minimalist, these gardens organize space in very different ways than Western-style gardens. Asian-inspired gardens usually feature water sources, dry landscapes with stones and gravel, and architectural (often dwarf) versions of trees and shrubs. ***Rock gardens,*** which mimic alpine mountainsides, are built on a vertical space and are the perfect garden solutions for a sloped yard. They feature low-growing flowers and foliage tucked around rocks. ***Water gardens*** often are part of other gardens, although frequently centerpieces. Some water gardens feature waterfalls to create musical sounds, as well as still areas where water lilies can grow. Bog areas around water gardens encourage marginal plants (those that like wet soil). Most water gardens also contain fish. (Koi is a popular choice.)

Vertical gardens are perfect for rooftop or small-space gardeners because plants are chosen for their upward growth capabilities. Vertical gardens use vines and columnar trees and shrubs. ***Heirloom gardens*** are where history meets horticulture. Heirloom gardens may simply feature old-fashioned plants, or they may focus on plants from a specific era or century.

Knot gardens are elements of a formal garden and feature low-growing plants in schemes that replicate knot shapes. Knot gardens generally are more structural than colorful and are very decorative. ***Parterre gardens*** are a French style of garden that feature low-growing plants—often very colorful—organized in beds that form patterns. Parterres generally are circular, square or rectangular.

Wildlife gardens are filled with flowers and berries and are usually informal. The plants are selected specifically to attract wildlife—birds, bees, butterflies—because they offer food, shelter or both. ***Woodland gardens*** are also called shade gardens and feature annuals and perennials that do well in low-light locations, as well as other woodland natives such as wildflowers and mosses.

Cacti and ornamental shrubs create a naturalistic garden style that builds interest from plant and stone textures rather than from an organized design or lots of flowers.

Trough Garden

Weathered-looking stone containers make handsome homes for alpine and small ornamental plants that may otherwise be swallowed up in a larger garden. You can buy a stone trough or make your own with a cement-sand-peat moss mix called hypertufa. Plants that are just the right size for a trough planter include alyssum, primula, armeria, mosses, saxifrage, sedum, thyme and dwarf conifers.

Knot Garden

A knot garden is a low-growing formal design planted so that the lines and curves of the plants create a knot pattern. The open space made by the intersections of the knot may be planted with a contrasting planting or filled in with mulch or gravel. A knot garden is a very controlled yet easy-to-grow garden and often is a focal point in a formal garden. Common plants found in knot gardens include lavender, boxwood, germander, thyme, lemon balm, rosemary and santolina.

Asian Garden

Gardens that incorporate Asian design elements are very popular. These naturalistic gardens use plants selected for texture and architecture. Weeping forms and dwarf varieties of trees and shrubs often are focal points. Mosses, thyme and baby's tears are used for groundcover texture. Water features—especially those that create soothing sounds—are common elements.

WHAT'S YOUR GARDENING STYLE?

Are you formal or informal? Should you buy old-fashioned heirloom varieties or the newest hybrids? Finding your garden style can help you figure out what types of plants, hardscaping elements and furniture you should buy for your garden. Take this quiz and see how you score!

1. What do you like to do most in your garden?
- A. Picking fresh flowers for bouquets
- B. Sitting in my garden and feeling close to nature
- C. Seeing the organizational structure of my garden
- D. A little bit of everything—cut flowers, grow vegetables, entertain friends

2. What colors do you like best?
- A. Soft pastel shades—especially yellows, pinks and purples
- B. Greens and subdued colors
- C. Bold, primary colors
- D. I love it all.

3. Which plant do you like the best?
- A. Sunflower
- B. Japanese maple
- C. Boxwood
- D. Cactus

4. What garden accents would you select?
- A. Old-fashioned signs, agricultural salvage, antiques
- B. Organic-looking items made from wood and stone
- C. A classic sundial or an urn
- D. Fun and funky "found art," modern sculpture

5. What shapes in a garden plan do you prefer?
- A. Loose, free-form curves
- B. Shapes that look natural, like they were just there instead of made
- C. Squares, rectangles and circles
- D. Irregular and asymmetrical shapes

6. Where would you rather go on vacation to see gardens?
- A. English countryside
- B. Far East
- C. A European castle or estate
- D. A sculpture garden outside a modern museum

If you picked mostly A: You like cottage style. The lush, flower-filled romantic feel of a cottage garden best suits you. Cottage gardens feature a mass—some might even call it a mess—of old-fashioned flowers that self-seed here and there. Cottage gardens are accented with antiques that capture the feeling of a past time. You derive a sense of exuberance from your garden.

If you picked mostly B: You like the look of a naturalistic garden. An Asian-style garden also falls into this category. You like organic materials such as stone and wood. These gardens take their cues from nature when it comes to design. You prefer stone pathways, unornamented wooden benches and other accents made from natural materials. You derive great peace from your garden.

If you picked mostly C: Formal garden style is for you. You like the sense of order and history that a formal garden conveys. Neatly clipped hedges, flowers that stay in their beds, classical ornaments that include urns and statuary—these are the elements that say "garden" to you. A formal garden makes you feel that there is order in the house (or yard!).

If you picked mostly D: You have a freeform contemporary style. This style is distinct and individualistic. Focal points often are pieces of contemporary art. Contemporary gardens feature geometric patterns in paving, and repetition in plantings. A contemporary style allows you to express your artistic self.

If you picked a mix of letters: Congratulations! You know what you like and you follow your own sense of style. You have what may be best described as personal style. This is the most freeing type of garden style because you can take what you love about all the styles and combine them in your garden.

Chapter Three
creating outdoor spaces

The area around your home offers lots of outdoor living options—an alfresco version of the inside of your home—with a dining area, kitchen, den and even cozy spot to take a nap.

create your own garden retreat

Your garden can be the place where you go to relax, regroup and catch up with your friends and family, but you need to create the right space to do that. Recasting your outdoor areas into living, dining and cooking space is easy when you follow the same rules that apply to the rooms inside your home.

Define garden space. Use a preexisting structure—a garage, shed or the back or side of your house—to create a wall for your outdoor room. If your room doesn't adjoin the house, add a freestanding wall, a hedge, or a lattice screen covered with a blooming vine to create space dividers. You can shape a room by adding a paved area or planting flower beds at the edges. Flooring also helps define space. Stone paving offers a smooth, even surface that looks good and is easy to maintain. Gravel is less formal and equally easy to care for. A fast and simple solution is to unroll an outdoor rug to instantly create a sense of definition. An outdoor space can be made to feel roomlike by the addition of an overhead structure. A flower-covered pergola, a retractable awning or a market umbrella all add physical structure overhead. For more ephemeral structure, a candelabra or chandelier strung from a tree can delineate the upward boundaries of a room.

Furnish it. Whether you live in an urban loft or a suburban house or have a place in the country, you can create outdoor living spaces right outside your back door by furnishing the area in the way that defines the room you want. If you're dreaming of a lounge area that's a place to kick back and relax, add comfy couches and deep-cushioned chairs. If you need a spot for a quiet hour of reading or snoozing, string up a hammock between two trees or add a daybed in the shade of a pergola. A dining area needs a table and seating appropriate for the number of people you routinely entertain. Size a table and chairs so they don't overwhelm or feel too small in an area. If you have a petite terrace, a bistro seat is perfect. If you have more space, a larger table (or two) can work. Even in the garden, a simple bench placed at the end of a pathway offers a destination—and a view.

Control your climate. Make your outdoor room usable in all seasons by providing climate control. Block harsh winds by planting trees or shrubs at the edges of your yard or outdoor living space. Cool down areas with shade from retractable awnings and market umbrellas. Outdoor ceiling fans installed on porches or pergolas keep the air moving so even the hottest evenings don't feel uncomfortable. (Plus, the flowing air often deters mosquitoes and other annoying insects.) Misting systems (either installed or freestanding) can cool down the summer heat with the flick of a switch. Most systems lower the ambient temperature of an area by 10 degrees. And when the temperatures drop, light up a patio-size chimenea or outdoor fireplace (either gas or wood-burning) to warm up. A freestanding or ceiling-mounted outdoor gas heater can take the chill off a cool evening and extend your entertaining time on both ends of summer.

Make it private. Your outdoor rooms can be made to feel more secluded in a number of ways. Hang curtains or fabric panels from a porch or pergola. Add screens or room dividers to block the view of a neighbor's yard. You can plant small trees in big containers and position them for maximum privacy. If you have large containers with flowers, place them on bases with casters to wheel them around to wherever you need a little privacy screening.

Make it colorful. The great advantage of having an outdoor room is that it's outside—and you can grow your own color around it. A frilly foundation planting of shrub roses offers gorgeous blooms and fabulous fragrance. Install window boxes and plant them full of cascading flowers. Suspend hanging baskets of blooms from house overhangs or from tree branches. Make use of vertical growers such as vines. As they grow up trellises on the sides of a house, they add color, flowers and fragrance.

creating rooms: dividers

It's a simple math problem. How do you create two spaces out of one? You divide, of course. Walls, fences and hedges all provide permanent ways to delineate and define the space in your yard. And there are temporary solutions, such as hanging curtains or setting up a freestanding screen, that allow you to create an intimate area in your garden.

Wonder Wall

Erect a freestanding wall to carve up the space in your yard. The white wooden wall (*top*) creates a sense of enclosure and privacy. In this shady space it also adds a brightening element.

Green Screen

Espaliered fruit trees bisect the yard (*right*) with green precision. Espalier is the method of training trees—through pruning and grafting—to grow flat against a structure such as a wall or, in this case, in a freestanding position. Espaliered plants create a focal point and a leafy divider in areas where space is limited.

Curtain Call

Sheer curtains or shower curtains (*bottom*) make great impromptu garden walls that seclude an area and create a theatrical sense of space.

Rosy Divider

A lattice fence with a scalloped top (*opposite*) offers an easy surface for a blush-pink climbing rose to cling to and climb up and over. Lattice screens or fencing make excellent garden room dividers because they allow airflow and light into all areas.

Laying the Groundwork: Floors

Flooring identifies and defines a garden room space from the ground up. Changing the material underfoot is the fastest way to say, "Step into my new room." Choose from rustic and replaceable mulches, or permanent options such as flagstone, brick or gravel. Or simply unfurl flooring for a temporary party by throwing down a couple of weather-resistant outdoor rugs directly on the lawn.

Stepping Out
Flooring can define an outdoor room's space even when nothing else identifies it as a room. Wood decking (*top*) surrounded by plant-edged concrete squares illustrates how to mix different flooring media for beautiful effect.

Rock On
River stone mosaics (*right*) add undulating interest to this outdoor area. For little surprises, leave planting pockets in stone or brick pathways and grow treadable (something you can walk on) groundcovers such as woolly thyme or Irish moss.

Roll Out Color
Weather-resistant outdoor area rugs instantly establish a space as a room. The 9×12-foot rug (*bottom*) covers the space while adding color, texture and coziness to the sitting area.

Mix It Up
Varying the type of stone used in paths and seating areas allows you to change the tone and texture of a space. Plus, thc beauty and ease of care of natural stone and rock make them excellent and versatile flooring options. A path (*opposite*) of formal mortared flagstone leads into a casual walkway of loose river rock, creating a new mood.

Defining Space Overhead: Ceilings

Create a sense of enclosure by topping off your outdoor room with a ceiling. Whether it's a permanent structure, such as a pergola with roses or low-hanging grape vines, or a large market umbrella to create shade, an overhead structure makes an outdoor room feel complete.

Pergola Perfection

A simple square structure in your yard creates the semblance of a room. The imposing black pergola (*above*) has an airy wire top (which could hold flowering vines) and see-through walls. Deep-seated furniture makes this a comfortable spot to relax with morning coffee or afternoon libations.

High-Wire Act

String wire between two structures and grow vines to create an overhead lattice of green. Wisteria vine (*right*) marches boldly from one end of the wire to the other.

Rain or Shine

Pop open a market umbrella (*below*) and you have instant ambience, as well as shade when you need it. Create a sense of ceiling by having more than one umbrella in your outdoor room. Look for materials in a wide range of colors that stand up to sun without fading. Some umbrellas tilt for added flexibility and can be lighted from within for nighttime dining.

Temporary Shade

With quick improvisation you can create a private outdoor alcove. Fabric allows you to create easy ceilings and walls for temporary events such as birthday or graduation parties. A striped rectangle of grommet-edged canvas (*opposite*) is suspended from four rustic twigs over a garden bench.

"My favorite summer activity is eating dinner with my kids at our backyard picnic table." —Susan

Dining Rooms: *This* is Eating Out!

What's more relaxing than eating outdoors? You don't have to worry about spilled drinks or pizza staining the carpet. And Mother Nature takes care of the ambience—the stars in the night sky overhead twinkle, garden flowers scent the air and butterflies flit from blossom to blossom. Creating an alfresco dining area in your yard turns every meal outdoors into a memorable event.

Make your outdoor dining area feel separate and special by delineating it from the rest of the garden. Narrow the entry path to create the feel of an anteroom that leads into a private dining area. Establish outer edges to the dining area by using stone or bricks to define the space. Or plant a border of fragrant plants such as rosemary or lavender. (Planting an edging of herbs also allows you to snip garnishes for iced teas and grilled meats and fish.) You also can add planters or tall plants at the outer corners of the garden to create a sense of privacy and enclosure.

LEFT A big table and a couple of rustic benches are all you need for outside dining. Use colorful linens for instant ambience (and a clean eating surface).

RIGHT From garden bed to tabletop, a salad of fresh greens and plump asparagus is the perfect alfresco side dish.

DINING ROOM: ELEMENTS

FOCAL POINT
A rectangular wooden pergola positioned at the rear of the yard offers a structural focal point.

PRIVACY
A row of dense arborvitae and taller deciduous trees screen the backyard from the neighboring home's view.

EDGING
The dining area is surrounded by fragrant lavender. A pair of square terra-cotta planters with Japanese holly (*Ilex crenata* 'Convexa') add detail and structure to the dining area.

AMPLE SPACE
This 18×22-foot space becomes a large dining area with defining decorative plantings. The round teak table seats six to eight diners.

Light Up the Night

Candlelight is an easy, economical and totally low-tech option for lighting outdoor meals. You don't need to run electricity to your dining area, and there are many fun ways for candles to light up the party. Candlelit chandeliers add instant romance (and lighting from overhead) to outdoor evening dinners. Add tabletop hurricane lamps for illumination on breezy evenings. Or why not install inground solar lights? They can be added anywhere that receives sunlight (just stick them in the ground) and cost nothing to run.

Set the Table

Choose a table that seats your usual number of guests. If you're going to use your garden dining room for early-morning coffee sipping while you do the crossword puzzle, a small, round bistro table may be all you need. If you plan to entertain outdoors for a group, get a long, rectangular table that can accommodate the number of guests you invite. You also can push two small tables together to create a larger one hidden under a large tablecloth. Round tables can seat more people than square tables, so keep that in mind as you decide on dining area furniture.

Serve in Style

Make your outdoor dining room as functional as the one inside your house. Set up drink stations or serving tables to allow you to stock refreshments and next courses without having to run back into the house. Ice-cold drinks refresh guests on the hottest summer evenings.

Pull Up a Seat

When it comes to seating options, consider comfort first. If you want to enjoy your outdoor spaces, cushioned and ample seating is a must. You'll have your pick of many durable materials: teak, hardwood, resin, aluminum. Choose the materials that fit your style and budget. And you can combine seating options—benches and couches mixed with single chairs, for example.

"With an outdoor kitchen I can cook while watching the kids play. Plus, I can grill veggies from the garden." —Barb

Kitchens: Cook in Your Garden

Outdoor cooking areas—more than just a place to set up a grill—is the hottest landscaping trend. And why not? Who wants to come in from the great outdoors to make and eat dinner inside? Having a kitchen outdoors means you can take the fresh produce from your garden and cook it up right on the spot. Food does not get any fresher than that.

Open-air kitchens—whether manufactured or custom-built—include all the amenities of indoor kitchens. Appliances are made from weather-resistant materials and are approved for outdoor use. Sleek stainless-steel smokers, grills and ovens make it possible for you to grill, cook and bake, just as indoors. Compact under-counter refrigerators chill food and drinks. There are even storage built-ins that allow you to keep table linens, candles and condiments handy for fast dinners.

Plan your outdoor kitchen around how you and your family like to cook and eat. And make sure your dining area is situated near the kitchen—just as it is in your home—for the ultimate ease in "eating out." If you install an outdoor kitchen in your yard, locate it near your house and you'll likely use it more often—especially in cooler weather.

There are a number of experts you'll need for installation: an electrician, a plumber and possibly a stonemason. But first contact contractors who have installed outdoor kitchens in your area and ask to talk with their clients about what they enjoy about their outdoor kitchens and how they use them.

LEFT Cook up something amazing in your own backyard. Add an outdoor kitchen to your landscaping and you'll enjoy more meals outdoors.

RIGHT Grilled corn for dinner is a snap when you have a kitchen in your backyard.

KITCHEN: ELEMENTS

COOKING SYSTEM
This state-of-the-art cooking system features a smoker, charcoal grill, gas grill and gas oven.

WORK SPACE
You can't have too many cooks in the kitchen when you're in the great outdoors. Ample counter space means more people can help out.

LIGHTING
Place task lights above or next to appliances and light paths to make it safe to cook after dark.

STONEWORK
Natural-looking stone facing around the appliances makes an outdoor kitchen feel like part of the landscape. Stone flooring distinguishes the work area from the lawn.

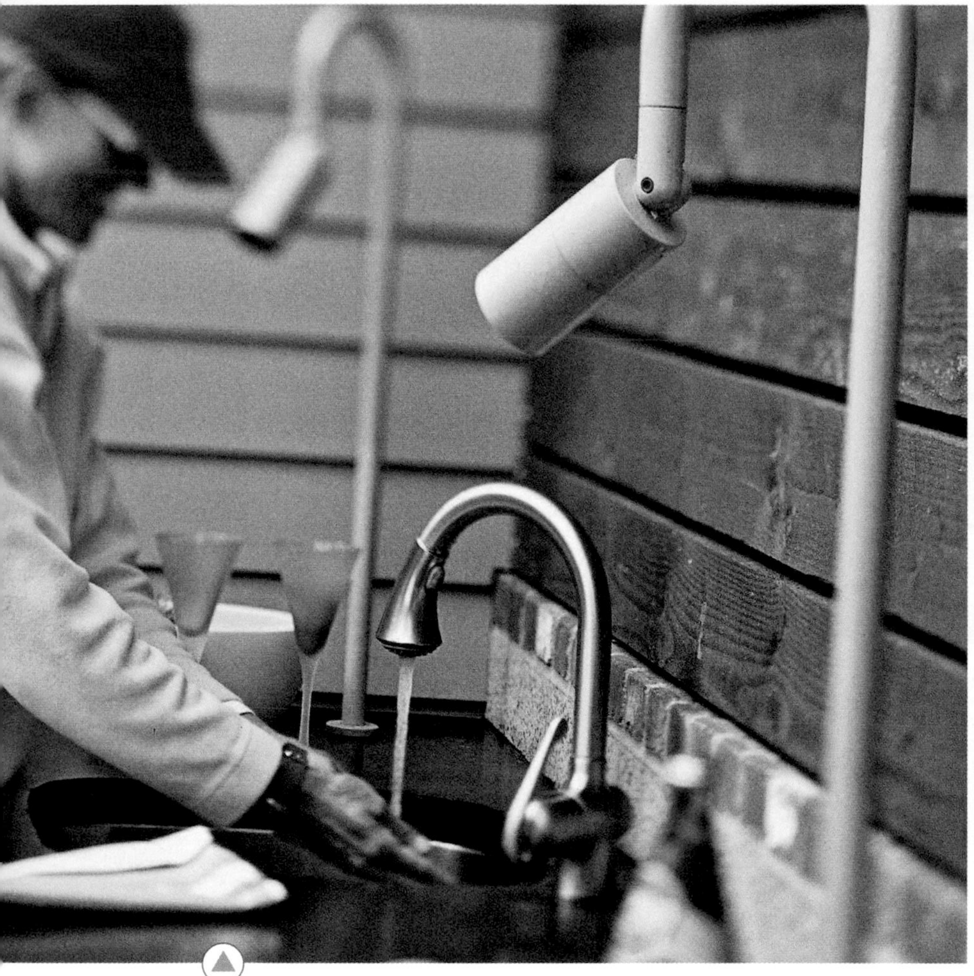

Wash Up

You'll use an outdoor sink more than you can ever imagine. It's an essential for food prep and cleanup. Don't skimp on the size—a bar-size sink may be too small for your needs. Choose one that's at least 20 inches wide and include a gooseneck faucet. If you have the room and resources, splurge on more than one sink.

Cut Up

An ample food prep area makes it easier to process food straight from the garden. Easy-clean cutting surfaces near a sink allow you to cook outdoors as easily as inside. If you have the space, plan for 2 to 3 feet of countertop. Bluestone and stainless steel repel stains well. Concrete is a popular choice, but freezing and thawing can cause cracks in cold climates.

Get Cooking

Cook like a pro. Smoke a turkey or grill a hot dog. You can have the power and versatility to cook however you like. Outdoor kitchens feature appliances you can't have indoors—like a smoker. Stainless-steel cladding stands up to the weather, and the domed top and ceramic-lined interior ensure that meats and fish are smoked evenly. For grilling purists add a charcoal grill, and for those who like push-button efficiency, add a gas grill. A gas-powered oven allows you to warm up bread, or bake a fresh berry pie for dessert.

Chill Out

An under-counter stainless-steel refrigerator keeps drinks icy cold and right at hand for gardeners, swimmers and backyard campers. Approved for outdoor use, these small coolers also keep fruit, salads and condiments properly chilled. Refrigerator drawers are another small-space cooling option.

"I like to entertain outdoors—and I want to offer my guests all the same comforts of indoors." —Hannah

Living Rooms: Kick Back and Relax

Outdoor spaces can be just as well-appointed and comfortable as indoor rooms—thanks in part to the availability of an amazing selection of outdoor décor items. Outdoor fabrics feature beautiful colors and designs. Created to stand up to sun and rain, these quick-to-dry fabrics are incredibly durable and easy to care for. You'll find fabrics for a wide assortment of decorative options: cushions, throw pillows, curtains, overhead sunscreens and umbrellas. The best thing about fabrics is you can change them quickly to create a new color theme.

Mildew-resistant outdoor rugs are cushy and decorative underfoot in sizes from throw-rug to full-room scale. You can unfurl them directly on the lawn for an impromptu room. Or cover up worn decking or plain concrete with rugs in a wide range of colors and styles.

Lighting in outdoor spaces has moved way beyond candlelight in the past several years. Wired for outdoor use, floor lamps with weatherproof fabric shades add an element of formality and provide a large amount of light. Try a simple lighting solution—overhead string lighting adds a sprinkling of electric starlight. Or position large, glass-enclosed hurricane lanterns on tabletops and at the room's entrance to offer romantic candlelight, even on windy nights.

Furniture for outdoor rooms is available in every style from traditional teak to cottage-garden-inspired all-weather wicker and contemporary colorful resin. For a look that mimics indoor sectionals, try outdoor modular deep-seating furniture that offers comfort as well as many possible arrangement options.

Dress up a plain pergola with red weatherproof curtains. Make straight-backed teak furniture more colorful and comfortable by adding deep-seating cushions.

LIVING ROOM: ELEMENTS

SHADE
A canvas market umbrella furnishes welcome shade on a sunny day.

FIREPLACE
A gas-powered or wood-burning fireplace creates warmth and ambience.

COMFORTABLE SEATING
Encourage guests to pull up a seat and stay awhile. Deep-cushioned seating lets you transform hardwood and metal furniture into cushy overstuffed chairs. Use weatherproof fabric, and it won't fade in the sun.

TABLES
Provide tables and end tables to hold drinks, food and outdoor decorative accessories.

FLOWERS AND FOLIAGE
Potted shrubs and trees create structure and offer shade and greenery. Plant trailing flowers at the base for added color.

Add Comfy Seats

Outdoor seating doesn't have to be expensive or elaborate—just comfortable. You can create spontaneous seating by laying down a grass mat and tossing down four cushions. Other comfortable living room seating includes chaise lounges (available in a wide range of styles and materials), hammocks and sling-back chairs.

Toast Marshmallows

An outdoor fireplace adds denlike ambience to an outdoor room. Whether you install a push-button gas fireplace or a wood-burning one, you'll enjoy the warmth and glow of a fire. You can go with a fire pit or chimenea, a smaller and less costly version.

Drape the Area

Make an outdoor room more intimate by adding indoor details such as curtains. Hang up sheer panels to define the area. Or grow your own natural drapes. In this photo a ledge above the door holds four pots of trailing ivies, whose tendrils are pulled back with fabric ties to look like foliage curtains.

Accessorize

Look in your garden shed to find furnishings to outfit your outdoor living room. A trio of birdbath bases become table legs, a lattice trellis morphs into a wall, and a grapevine wreath turns into the frame for a mirror.

Chapter Four

easy Garden Plans

Grow a garden! Here are 23 gorgeous gardens with everything you need to plant them yourself—plans, plant lists and accessories.

Create Your Dream Garden

A garden is an investment in your future happiness. Making a garden is like making a cake. You start with a recipe (the garden plan) and add the ingredients (the plants).

Jump in with passion. If you've never planted a garden before, you'll discover that gardening is like other sorts of DIY projects—cooking, crafts, sewing. You start with a plan, you gather your materials and you dig in. (And with gardening, this is literally true.) Keep in mind that no matter where you live and no matter what type of soil, light and water conditions exist in your yard, you can have a beautiful garden.

Set the magic in motion. When you plan and plant a garden, you're starting something that will play out in its own way. A garden is like a windup toy. You crank it and stand back and see what happens next. Some plants will grow—with great exuberance—and spill out of the place you planted them. And some plants may die. (Most of the time this will have had little to do with your care and be more about your environment.) The trick is to find the plants that love your yard's conditions and plant them for their lovely foliage and floral rewards.

Draw up a plan. A garden plan is like a road map. You are here—headed in a specific direction. This guide shows you the shape of the garden and the plants that go within each part. The plans in this book have been created to present a variety of options and types of plants. If you find a plant in a plan that doesn't work in your zone, you can replace it with another plant that does.

Watch and learn. Garden plans are all about creating a series of relationships—plants that bloom at the same time, such as roses and clematis; leaves that complement each other, such as hostas and ferns; plants that just look good together. Once you've had success with pairing plants you can take that knowledge and make other gardening relationships. This is the art and creativity of gardening.

Capitalize on plant timing. Paying attention to bloom season helps you anticipate your garden's changing look. Perennials and bulbs bloom on a time clock. Annuals bloom all summer. Take the natural talents of these plant groups and show them off in your garden. Gardeners who want continuous flower color plant perennials and bulbs for their timed blooms, and they use annuals to fill in the blanks.

Be fearless. Don't be afraid to move or cut back plants. Sometimes, perennial plants need a better site, so dig them up and replant them in a more suitable location. Cut back perennials when they start looking scruffy; you won't hurt them and you may get a second round of blooms. As your garden grows you may notice things you want to change. For example, a common but easy-to-fix problem in a perennial border is one successful plant that overtakes other plants. Easy spreaders are a gardener's best friend until they overstep their boundaries. (A list of perennials that don't have brakes and will quickly fill in all open spots—depending on your zone and growing conditions—often includes mint, perennial sunflower, lily of the valley and ribbon grass.) If a specific plant gets too big, you can dig out a portion of it and pass it along to other gardening friends. You also can plant the spreader in a place where it can grow rampant and look great. Or you can remove it altogether. It's your garden, and you decide how it looks.

Replicate your successes. Take notes throughout the growing season, jotting down what color or bloom combinations appeal to you. You might see how the arching fronds of bleeding heart drape across the puckered leaves of the hosta. If you like this combination, try other plant combinations that exhibit the same growth habits. If you discover a look that really appeals to you, mimic it in another place in your yard.

"I want a romantic and unstructured garden with lots of gorgeous flowers for bouquets." —Cassandra

Old-Fashioned Gardens: For the Love of Flowers

The cottage garden is, for many, the classic English-style garden. The design is informal—some may even say messy. Beds are densely planted with masses of flowers, giving the garden a very full, casual look. Many cottage gardens are enclosed—which makes them by design excellent options for entryways. In fact a colorful cottage garden says a joyous "Welcome!" to visitors in a way a simple line of yews or other evergreen shrubs just doesn't.

For the gardener who can't decide on a favorite flower, a cottage garden is a must. A cottage garden is a feast for the senses. You can plant about any type of flower in a cottage garden, as well as edible herbs (such as creeping thyme and rosemary), as well as plants that are native to your area (such as ornamental grasses). Cottage gardens impose no rules when it comes to plant selection—if you like it, you should plant it! Although there are some traditional cottage garden plantings—including back-of-border beauties such as foxgloves and delphiniums, or petite pansies that bloom along the garden's edge—this is a garden that truly embodies the adage "The more, the merrier." Roses also play a big role in the romance of a cottage garden, especially the big "cabbage-headed" roses that look so beautiful paired with other flowers and as cut flowers in bouquets. Many roses are also fragrant; another plus.

Common architectural elements in a cottage garden include fences (often white picket or rustic wood), which create a sense of boundary for these otherwise rangy spaces. Arbors are used as entryways and are often smothered with flowering vines such as clematis or climbing roses. An arbor can be a simple arch, or an ornate archway with a gate. Other structural elements of a cottage garden include pathways and benches.

If you love flowers—a lot of flowers—then a cottage garden is for you. Abundant and colorful, a cottage garden teems with blooms from spring to autumn.

Arbors

A structure adds a focal point to a cottage garden, and the quintessential cottage garden structure is the arbor. Used as an entry portal or as a way to connect one garden to another, an arbor adds height too. An arbor can be a simple arch, have some depth to it or sometimes even provide seating. There are many types of materials to use, from rustic tree boughs to stylish wood. And for a low-maintenance option (read: no painting!), you can get molded plastic.

ABOVE A white picket fence and matching arbor are the perfect pair for a cottage garden. A fence creates a sense of boundary. It's also a structure upon which climbing plants can entwine.

LEFT Iron arches make sturdy arbors for heavy climbers such as roses and trumpet vine. Create an inviting walkway through a series of arches leading to a garden focal point, in this case a container filled with elephant ears.

OPPOSITE Heap on the flowers! An arched arbor smothered with climbing roses makes a gorgeous and fragrant garden entryway. Keep it low maintenance: Don't paint the arbor if you're planning to have a vine climb on it. That way you won't have to cut back the vine when the wood needs another coat.

COTTAGE GARDEN FLOWERS A to Z

Aster
Bergamot, Borage
Cornflower, Campion
Daisy, Delphinium
Euphorbia
Forget-Me-Not
Goldenrod, Geranium
Hollyhock, Hyssop
Impatiens
Jacob's-ladder
Kiss-Me-Over-The-Garden-Gate (*Polygonum orientale*)
Larkspur, Lavender
Mignonette, Mallow
Nepeta (Catmint)
Oxeye Daisy
Poppy, Pansy
Queen Anne's Lace
Rhododendron
Sweet Rocket, Sweet William
Thyme
Valerian, Viola
Wild Pansy, Wild Poppy
Yarrow
Zantedeschia (Calla Lily)

'Redouté'

Old Roses With New Tricks

Roses are the spirit of romance, which is why they are included in so many cottage garden plans. They range in color from deep red to blush pink, soft yellow or snow white. David Austin English roses are sheer exuberance in flower form. These roses combine the flowers and fragrances of old roses but they also offer the repeat flowering characteristic of modern versions. David Austin English roses are easy to grow and reliable. These petal-packed roses mix well with perennials and shrubs. Grow these romantic roses for gorgeous garden blooms and bountiful bouquets.

'Gertrude Jekyll'

'Abraham Darby'

Roses are excellent garden minglers. Heavy-headed English roses bow into a mixed perennial border planted with perky shasta daisies and purple monkshood.

Delphinium + Nasturtium

Dynamic Duos

A cottage garden may appear to be an unplanned frenzy of blooms, but there is some method to the madness. Creating such a casual look requires a little artistic matchmaking. Although a cottage garden is informal, it should be full of small surprises. And one of those surprises is planting partner vignettes—pairings of plants whose flower types and colors complement each other. Roses and lilies are a classic cottage duo because they bloom at the same time and their flower forms are so different. Delphinium, one of the grande dames of the cottage garden, looks great with mounded nasturtiums in red and yellow.

Phlox + Coneflower

Lily + Rose

Daisy + Clematis

Hollyhock + Black-Eyed Susan

Foxglove + Dianthus

Peony + Foxglove

Picket Fence Cottage Border

A mix of colors and textures gives a cottage garden its *joie de vivre*. The backdrop of a wall or fence gives the border structure.

Cranesbill Geranium

Lavender

Snapdragon

Veronica

- **A.** **1 David Austin Rose** *(Rosa* 'Mary Rose') Zones 5-9
- **B.** **1 David Austin Rose** *(Rosa* 'Tea Clipper') Zones 5-9
- **C.** **5 Common Foxglove** *(Digitalis purpurea)* Zones 4-8
- **D.** **1 Cranesbill** *(Geranium* spp.) Zones 3-9, depending on species
- **E.** **1 Lavender** *(Lavandula angustifolia)* Zones 5-8
- **F.** **1 *Verbena* x *hybrida*** Zones 4-8
- **G.** **1 Veronica** *(Veronica* spp.) Zones 3-11, depending on species
- **H.** **5 Snapdragon** *(Antirrhinum majus)* Zones 5-9
- **I.** **3 Golden Calla** *(Zantedeschia elliottiana)* Zones 9-10

PLANT PROFILE

FOXGLOVE

THE BELLE OF THE BORDER

The foxglove (*Digitalis purpurea*) is a tall plant that blooms every other year. (This type of plant is called a biennial.) It is hardy in zones 4 to 9 and grows a fantastic 4 to 6 feet tall. It does best in partial shade. To get your foxglove to bloom twice a summer, cut off spent blooms. After the second bloom, leave the flower heads intact so that they can self-seed.

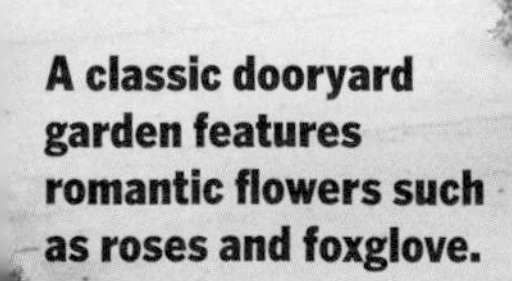

A classic dooryard garden features romantic flowers such as roses and foxglove.

Corner Garden Border

Add an old-fashioned floral flourish at the edges of your yard with this easy-to-plant corner garden.

Gloriosa Daisy

Moss Rose

Cosmos

Butterfly Bush

- **A. 9 Moss Rose** (*Portulaca grandiflora*) Zones 9-11, annual elsewhere
- **B. 9 Narrow-Leaf Zinnia** (*Zinnia angustifolia*) Annual
- **C. 12 Dusty Miller** (*Senecio cineraria* 'Silver Dust') Zones 8-11, annual elsewhere
- **D. 2 *Petunia* x *hybrida*** Annual
- **E. 6 Flowering Tobacco** (*Nicotiana alata*) Annual
- **F. 12 *Cosmos bipinnatus*** Annual
- **G. 4 Gloriosa Daisy** (*Rudbeckia hirta* 'Irish Eyes') Zones 3-7
- **H. 2 Feather Reed Grass** (*Calamagrostis* x *acutiflora*) Zones 4-9
- **I. 3 *Penstemon* 'Maurice Gibbs'** Zones 7-10, annual elsewhere
- **J. 1 Butterfly Bush** (*Buddleja davidii* 'Nanho Blue') Zones 5-9
- **K. 7 Spider Flower** (*Cleome hassleriana*) Annual
- **L. 1 Speedwell** (*Veronica longifolia* 'Fairytale') Zones 4-8

PLANT PROFILE

CLEOME

OLD-FASHIONED BLOOMS

Tall and dramatic, annual cleome (*Cleome hassleriana*) towers over the summer garden. Also called spider flower, cleome grows 4 feet tall and produces large balls of flowers with spidery seedpods. Cleome self-seeds prolifically, so you only have to plant it once. Cleome does best in moderately rich, well-drained soil. Group in clusters of six or more for best effect.

A small flowerbed takes just an afternoon to plant. In six to eight weeks you'll enjoy a lush and colorful garden—all the way to frost.

"I don't get home until after 5pm and I want a garden I can enjoy in the evening." —Gwen

Night Gardens: After-Dark Delights

An 8-to-5 job can put a crimp in your summer outdoor living time. If you work during the day, you may feel that you are missing out on your garden's glory. After all, what's more beautiful than a flower-filled garden on a sunny day? But you can enjoy a gorgeous garden, even after the sun goes down. How? By adding glow-in-the-dark plants to your landscape. Night gardens, sometimes called moon gardens, are designed to look beautiful, even after dark.

A wide range of flowers and foliage plants can literally light up your garden. White and light-colored flowers glow from beds and borders. And variegated foliage plants also offer splashes of light, which look more pronounced in the evening. White-flowering or light-foliaged shrubs can turn on the lights in your landscape.

Night garden plants also look great in the sunshine. But many have special talents that make them especially beautiful at night. For example, the large, pendulous blooms of angels' trumpets, also called brugmansia, appear to float in the darkness because their green stems and leaves fade into the night. And white impatiens edging a garden path create a soft footlight effect that makes the walkway a bit more visible at dusk.

Many plants mysteriously take on new life after dark. In fact some can only be enjoyed after hours. Moonflowers, an annual vine related to the morning glory, bloom only at night. During the day, moonflower buds are tightly closed, but once the sun goes down, they open into large, white disks that measure 4 to 6 inches across. And if you have a water garden or pond, you can choose water lilies that bloom only at night.

Lighting, white accents and white- and light-colored flowers and foliage make an outdoor dining area more visually appealing after the sun goes down.

Glow-in-the-Dark Garden

Turn on the lights in a small garden by planting white and light-colored flowers of different heights. Add seating close by to enjoy the after-hours flower show.

Sweet Violet | Trailing Petunia | New Guinea Impatiens | Daisy 'Becky'

A. **2 Sweet Violet** (*Viola odorata*) Zones 8-9, annual elsewhere
B. **4 Trailing Petunia** (*Calibrachoa* x *hybridaiola odorata*) Annual
C. **1 Zinnia** (*Zinnia elegans* 'Peter Pan White') Annual
D. **1 Impatiens** (New Guinea Group) Annual
E. **3 Marigold** (*Tagetes*) Annual
F. **2 Iris** (*Iris germanica* 'Immortality') Zones 4-10
G. **2 Daisy** (*Leucanthemum* 'Becky') Zones 4-9

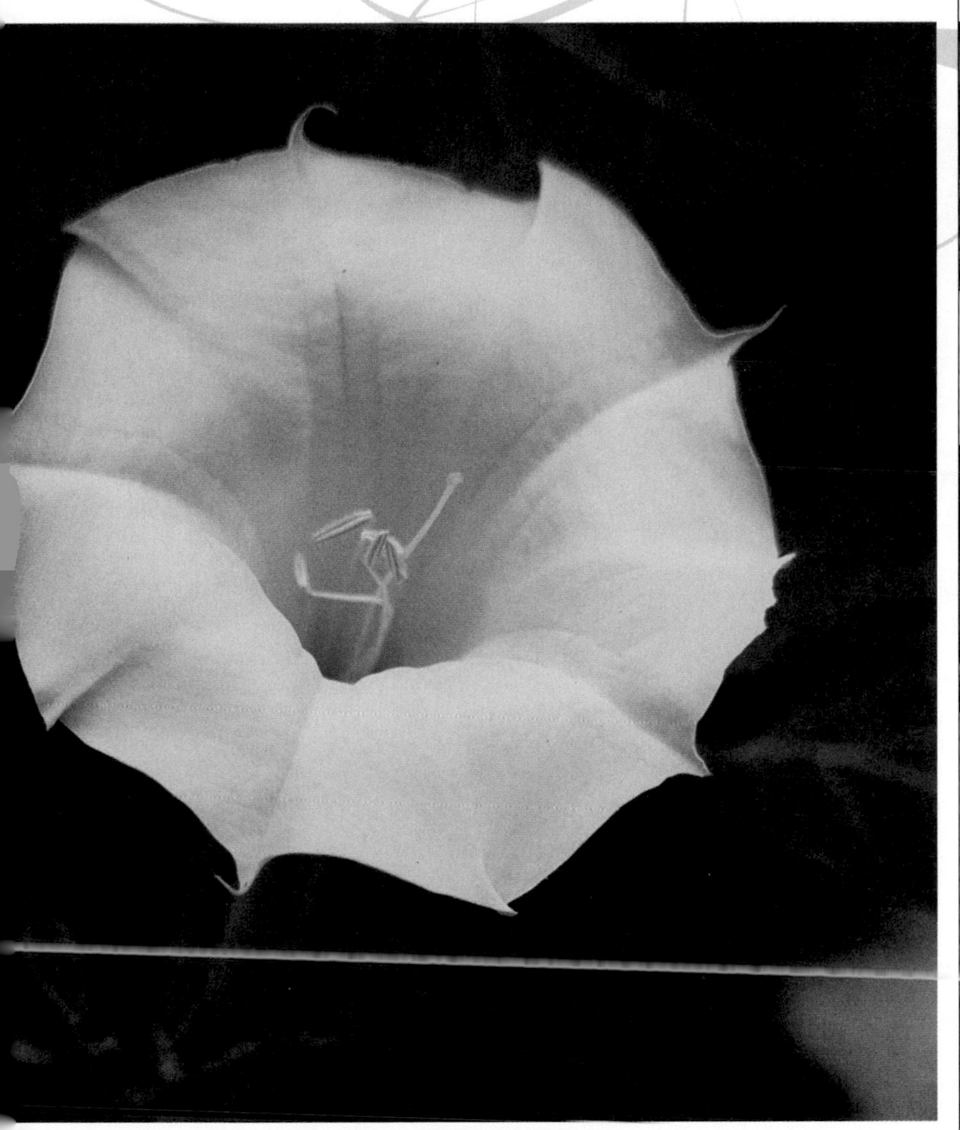

LUMINOUS BLOOMER

The large, trumpetlike blooms of datura (*Datura stramonium*) are showstoppers. This shrubby tender perennial (which grows as an annual in places that get frost) has gray-green leaves and large tubular, upward-facing flowers that bloom in white, yellow, pink and light purple. All are bright choices for night gardens. The fast-growing plant reaches 3 to 5 feet in height and is covered with handsome white flowers. It blooms all summer long. Datura produces round, spike-covered seeds—hence its common name, thorn apple. All parts of the plant are poisonous, so it's best not planted where there will be pets or small children.

NIGHT OWLS

Some flowers perform best after the sun goes down. Here are several you won't want to miss:

FOUR O'CLOCKS
You can't set your watch by these plants, but in the late afternoon, the perky blooms of four o'clocks (*Mirabalis jalapa*) open up.

PEACOCK ORCHID
Plant the quarter-size bulbs of peacock orchid, also called acidanthera (*Gladiolus callianthus*), in late spring and you'll enjoy these wonderfully fragrant flowers all summer. They grow well in containers—a good choice for northern gardeners because these tender bulbs must be stored inside for the winter, like dahlias or cannas.

MOONFLOWER
The moonflower (*Ipomoea alba*) is an annual vine that produces 4- to 6-inch brilliant-white blooms. During the day the flowers are closed in a tight swirl and resemble a long dollop of soft-serve ice cream. After dark the buds gently unfurl, revealing gorgeous flowers that scent the area with sweet perfume.

Light Up the Night

Creative outdoor lighting can enhance your garden, making it a relaxing and romantic haven after dark. And because a night garden is cloaked in darkness, an important safety element is a well-lit path. Easy-to-install outdoor lighting is available in energy-efficient solar and low-voltage options.

EASY DOES IT

Use a watertight timer that plugs into a standard exterior outlet to turn your outdoor lighting system on at the time you desire—and turn it off to coincide with the time you go to bed.

HOW TO INSTALL LOW-VOLTAGE LIGHTING

1. ATTACH CABLE Turn off the current. Separate the wires on the end of the electric cable. The wires go beneath the screws on the transformer. Follow the manufacturer's instructions.

2. POSITION THE LIGHTS Place them along a path or at the edge of a garden bed—wherever you want light.

3. DIG A TRENCH Dig about 5 inches down. Insert the cable into the trench and backfill the dirt that was removed.

4. PLUG IN THE TRANSFORMER Check that all your lights work. Low voltage lights are difficult to see in the daytime, so you may want to do this at dusk.

5. SET UP LIGHTS Take care to make sure all are straight. Use backfill soil to position them securely in the ground.

6. USE A TIMER Most transformers can be set to turn your lights on for morning and evening illumination.

"My neighborhood has watering restrictions. I need a garden that's not thirsty." —Kelly

Drought-Resistant Gardens: Low Maintenance and Beautiful

Plants are built to thrive in their native environments. And plants that originated in dry and arid places have developed special survival skills to stand up to drought conditions. Some have deep root systems that dig into the soil below the surface, where moisture hides. Others have developed fleshy tubers that store water for sustaining themselves in long rainless seasons. And some plants protect themselves from heat and drying winds with a shield of waxy or fuzzy leaves that helps hold in the moisture.

Drought-tolerant plants have evolved to live on little and sporadic watering. If you live in an arid climate or just don't want to water your garden on a regular basis, a drought-tolerant planting design is the perfect solution. Keep in mind that no plant can survive without any water, and it's especially important to keep your newly planted plants well watered until they are fully established in your landscape.

You may think that most drought-tolerant plants are monochromatic and spiny—and some are. But many have beautiful, vibrantly colored flowers that will look great in any garden. Purple coneflowers, ruby-red sedum and blazing-yellow rudbeckia are all garden favorites and are all stingy when it comes to their water consumption. And ornamental grasses, now more popular than ever, are excellent options for low-water, low-maintenance gardening.

When the heat kicks in, lavender stands its ground. This water-stingy plant blooms all summer and scents the air with its heady fragrance.

DROUGHT-RESISTANT GARDENS: DESIGN PLAN

Carefree Border

Self-sufficient plants that don't need constant care and watering make having a garden easier than ever.

- **A.** **2 Aspen** (*Populus* spp.) Zones 2-8
- **B.** **3 Lavender** (*Lavandula angustifolia*) Zones 5-8
- **C.** **2 Chinese Silvergrass** (*Miscanthus sinensis*) Zones 4-9
- **D.** **2 Russian Sage** (*Perovskia atriplicifolia*) Zones 6-9
- **E.** **10 Hardy Ice Plant** (*Delosperma cooperi*) Zones 8-10
- **F.** **9 Cosmos** (*Cosmos sulfureus*) Annual
- **G.** **20 Johnny-Jump-Up** (*Viola tricolor*) Zones 4-8
- **H.** **15 Sweet Alyssum** (*Lobularia maritima* 'Minima') Annual
- **I.** **20 Thyme** (*Thymus serpyllum* 'Minor' and *Thymus lanuginosus*) Zones 4-9
- **J.** **7 Blue Fescue** (*Festuca glauca* 'Sea Urchin') Zones 4-8
- **K.** **6 Siberian Iris** (*Iris sibirica* 'Caesar's Brother') Zones 3-8
- **L.** **6 Red-Hot Poker** (*Kniphofia uvaria*) Zones 6-9
- **M.** **3 Pincushion Flower** (*Scabiosa columbaria* 'Pink Mist') Zones 3-8
- **N.** **3 Lily** (*Lilium* 'Imperial Silver') Zones 3-9
- **O.** **1 *Sedum* 'Autumn Joy'** Zones 3-10
- **P.** **2 Speedwell** (*Veronica liwanensis*) Zones 4-9
- **Q.** **2 Cup Flower** (*Nierembergia* spp.) Zones 7-10
- **R.** **1 Sacred Datura** (*Datura meteloides*) Zones 10-11
- **S.** **5 Lavandin** (*Lavandula x intermedia*) Zones 5-8
- **T.** **1 Rocky Mountain Juniper** (*Juniperus scopulorum*) Zones 4-7
- **U.** **1 Rosemary** (*Rosmarinus officinalis* 'Arp') Zones 8-10

ROBUST AND DROUGHT RESISTANT

Sedums are very drought tolerant. The 18-inch-tall 'Autumn Joy' sedum is a beautiful border plant that is gorgeous when planted en masse. Growing in a thick clump, this plant produces chartreuse flower umbels that open to rosy-rust-colored flowers in late fall. Butterflies love these flowers. And if you don't like to water your garden, this plant is for you. Sedums thrive in full sun.

Drought-tolerant flowers allow you to plant your garden and forget about it.

Maiden Grass

Ornamental Grasses

Ornamental grasses are some of the most versatile plants in the garden. They offer a wide range of textures and colors and come in small to tall forms. Best of all, they lend interest in all seasons. In early spring the shoots rise from the ground. By summer the plants are full and shrubby. In fall, even after frost, they stand tall. And in winter the plumes offer architectural interest after frost has felled the rest of the garden.

Purple Fountain Grass

Japanese Forest Grass

A garden filled with ornamental grasses is textural and kinetic. On a breezy day, grasses move like waves in the wind.

EASY DOES IT

Plant these self-sufficient species and your watering tasks will be greatly reduced.

GRAY-GREEN FOLIAGE
Artemisia
Lamb's Ears

ORANGE- AND YELLOW-FLOWERING
Butterfly Weed
Bishop's Weed
Coreopsis
Daylily
Gaillardia
Goldenrod
Red-Hot Poker

BLUE- AND PURPLE-FLOWERING
Catmint
Lamb's Ears
Lavender
Purple Coneflower
Russian Sage

Plant masses of blooms to create a lush garden that looks great and also chokes out weeds.

HOW TO USE LESS WATER IN THE GARDEN

1. MULCH Add a 2- to 3-inch layer of mulch to help retain water and reduce evaporation. An added bonus: You'll weed less.

2. USE A SOAKER HOSE Water only when the soil is dry. A soaker hose or drip irrigation system allows you to deep-water your plants without losing hydration to evaporation.

3. COLLECT WATER A rain barrel allows you to catch rainfall and use it later.

4. IMPROVE YOUR SOIL Add compost or other organic material to your soil to help it retain moisture.

5. REDUCE THE SIZE OF YOUR LAWN Plant native grasses or low-water groundcovers such as creeping thyme.

6. MOW LOWER Set your mower blade at 3 inches or higher. And keep your blade sharp; Dull blades can increase water loss in your grass.

"I plant lots of flowers, and the birds and butterflies love my garden as much as I do." —Janie

Nature Gardens: Welcome Wildlife

Every garden is attractive to birds and butterflies, but there is a secret to luring in many different winged species. A garden designed with the needs and preferences of butterflies and birds will attract them—and it will become a place where they love to hang out. By planting food (nectar-rich blossoms), providing a water source (a shallow dish is all it takes) and shelter from the wind (trees and shrubs), you'll enjoy large numbers of visitors to your garden in all seasons.

Start with a garden site that receives full sun—southern exposure is best. Butterflies don't like wind, so a sheltered area is preferred. A wall or hedge creates a wind barrier so these featherweight insects can sip and sup without being buffeted. Birds also like a place that offers shelter—and a quick getaway perch from predators such as hawks or cats. A shrub backdrop is a great way to provide protection as well as privacy for your bird and butterfly garden.

The best way to attract the most species is to offer a variety of plants that are in flower from spring through fall. Butterflies seem to prefer hot-colored plantings—flowers that bloom in purple, red and orange. They flock to several well-known favorites. Butterfly bush and butterfly weed are favorites (no surprise), as are tithonia and zinnia. Hummingbirds love nectar-filled flowers too. They prefer blooms that are tubular or cup-shaped to accommodate their long, thin bills. Favorites include penstemon, delphinium, bee balm, columbine and butterfly bush.

LEFT Butterflies and birds love to dine on the sweet nectar of flowers. Creating a garden bed filled with their favorites will ensure that they'll visit often all season.

RIGHT Hummingbirds prefer red, trumpet-shaped flowers with lots of nectar.

Butterfly Buffet Border

Plants of varying heights offer a smorgasbord of feeding options for birds and butterflies.

Agastache

Columbine

Coneflower

Sedum

- **A.** 3 ***Agastache*** Zones 6-9
- **B.** 3 **Columbine** (*Aquilegia*) Zones 3-9
- **C.** 1 **Butterfly Bush** (*Buddleja davidii* 'Harlequin') Zones 6-9
- **D.** 2 **Butterfly Bush** (*Buddleja davidii* 'Royal Red') Zones 6-9
- **E.** 9 **Bellflower** (*Campanula cochlearifolia* 'Bavarian Blue') Zones 5-9
- **F.** 2 ***Caryopteris* x *clandonensis*** 'Longwood Blue' Zones 6-9
- **G.** 6 **Tickseed** (*Coreopsis grandiflora* 'Sunray') Zones 4-9
- **H.** 6 **Delphinium** (*Delphinium* 'King Arthur') Zones 4-7
- **I.** 3 **Coneflower** (*Echinacea purpurea* 'Magnus') Zones 3-9
- **J.** 3 **Bee Balm** (*Monarda* 'Raspberry Wine') Zones 4-8
- **K.** 3 **Penstemon** (*Penstemon barbatus* 'Nana Rondo') Zones 4-9
- **L.** 4 **Sedum** (*Sedum* x 'Vera Jameson') Zones 4-9
- **M.** 2 **Spike Speedwell** (*Veronica spicata* 'Alba') Zones 3-8
- **N.** 4 **Spike Speedwell** (*Veronica spicata* 'Goodness Grows') Zones 3-8

BUTTERFLY FAVORITE

This large shrubby plant, *Buddleja davidii,* has the common name butterfly bush because its alluring nectar brings in many different species of butterflies. Monarchs and swallowtails find the large sprays of blooms irresistible. On a hot, windless day it's not uncommon to find multiple butterflies feeding on this gorgeous bush. Also called summer lilac, this 4- to 6-foot-tall shrub produces sprays of tiny purple, pink or white flowers that are borne on gracefully arching branches.

Bright-red monarda and purple plumes of agastache lure butterflies for a sweet feast.

High Rise

An elevated freestanding water source is perfect for thirsty birds. Birdbaths should be 3 inches at the deepest point so birds can easily step in and bathe. Birdbaths should also feature sloping sides. A perch along the top lets birds lean in to take a drink. If there is the possibility of cats visiting your yard, find a safe, open spot to position your birdbath.

Fresh and Bubbly

Birds flock to the sound of moving water because it's fresher, so a birdbath with a circulating fountain is certain to be a draw. Make sure to add fresh water every other day or so. Dump out old water and brush away any growing algae to keep the birdbaths fresh and inviting.
Set the bath near a tree with overhanging branches so birds have a place to fly to quickly after bathing.

WINGED WONDERS

Enjoy the fabulous flitting of busy hummingbirds by planting a garden filled with their favorites. Hummingbirds feed by sight and prefer bright blooms. They are curious birds and will check out your garden as soon as flowers are blooming. Select a variety of plants (both annuals and perennials) that bloom from spring to frost and you'll be rewarded with birds throughout the season. Avoid using pesticides around hummingbird plants because these tiny birds might ingest poisons sprayed onto flowers.

GIVE HUMMERS A SWEET TREAT

Hummingbirds love brightly colored tubular blooms and are especially drawn to red flowers.

SALVIA
Easy-to-grow red salvia (*Salvia splendens*) loves lots of sun. Plant en masse (6 to 12 plants) to create a feast for flyby hummingbirds.

BEE BALM
The common name for *Monarda didyma*, this ruffled flower attracts ruby-throated hummingbirds from miles around. Tousled flower heads bloom in raspberry, white, red and violet.

HONEYSUCKLE
This flower grows in vine or shrub form. *Lonicera sempervirens* thrives just about anywhere in the United States.

"I don't have time or space for a big garden, but I want lots of flowers and some veggies." —Alexandria

Containers: Little Gardens Everywhere

Flowers everywhere you want them: That's what you get when you plant your garden in pots instead of in the ground. Container gardening levels the playing field, so to speak. You don't have to have a big yard or lots of land. You can plant a container garden anywhere including your front porch, your back patio or a balcony 12 stories up.

Containers are a versatile way to garden because you can control the variables namely soil, sunlight and garden location. Fill your containers with a well-balanced potting soil (some mixes even include fertilizer) and you won't have to worry about the pH or plantibility in your yard. And because you can place containers where you want them, you can choose a sunny area for vibrant annuals, such as geraniums, petunias and marigolds, or a container in the shade for colorful caladium, begonias and impatiens.

Container gardening is easy and offers endless outdoor décor possibilities. Containers come in every size, color and material. Go classic with basic terra-cotta, or choose brightly colored ceramic or plastic. Metal containers can be made from lightweight (and easy-to-move) aluminum, or they can be constructed from heavier zinc or iron. From large urns that flank a front doorway to shallow tabletop trough gardens, there's a container that will enhance every part of your yard and garden.

Annuals are popular planting choices for containers because they stay in bloom all summer and require little care—just add water. But you also can plant perennials such as swaying ornamental grasses or tall sprays of fragrant lavender. And you can think big by potting up small shrubs and trees. Containers allow you to expand your gardening horizons by growing exotic plants, including bananas or citrus, in climates where they wouldn't normally thrive. (Of course you need to move these tender beauties indoors when cold weather sets in.)

A springtime bowl of pansies, lettuce and chives make a great spring brunch centerpiece.

Classical Container Combo

One container is gorgeous, so a group of them is fantastic! Classic-shaped urns feature red hydrangeas for a showy display.

Bigleaf Hydrangea | Geranium | Hen-and-Chickens | Dichondra 'Silver Falls'

- **A. 2 Bigleaf Hydrangea** (*Hydrangea macrophylla* 'Pia') Zones 6-9
- **B. 1 Rose** (*Rosa* 'Anne Boleyn') Zones 5-9
- **C. 2 Geranium** (*Pelargonium* spp.) Zones 10-11, annual elsewhere
- **D. 2 Wandering Jew** (*Tradescantia zebrina*) Zones 9-11, annual elsewhere
- **E. 2 *Sedum sieboldii*** Zones 6-9
- **F. 2 Begonia** 'Pink Minx' Zones 10-11, annual elsewhere
- **G. 6 Hen-and-Chickens** (*Sempervivum tectorum*) Zones 4-8
- **H. 1 *Dichondra* 'Silver Falls'** Zones 9-11, annual elsewhere
- **I. 1 Silver Spear** (*Astelia chathamica* 'Silver Spear') Zones 8-10, annual elsewhere

SHOWY CENTERPIECE

If you're looking for a big, spiky plant to add a little height and drama to a container, try a phormium (*Phormium tenax*). These impressive plants bear a fountain of gorgeous straplike foliage, and they come in many different colors, from green to burgundy and yellow-striped. They grow in zones 9 to 10 but can be moved indoors in colder climates. (Plant in a container that's not too heavy to haul into a garage or down basement stairs.) Phormium's spearlike leaves offer textural punctuation to containers that are otherwise filled with low-growing or round-leafed plants.

Planting small hydrangeas in containers makes an instant impact.

Make a big impact with small elements. Stair-step three containers for a lush and colorful entryway planting.

PLANT PROFILE
SWEET POTATO VINE

CAREFREE TRAILER

Sweet potato vine (*Ipomoea batatas*) is a relative of the morning glory and will climb on a trellis or scamper across the ground, depending on how you want to use it. In a container it spills over the sides with wild abandon. Heart-shaped leaves come in several colors: for dark chocolate, try 'Blackie,' which does well in full sun to light shade; 'Marguerite' offers lush, chartreuse leaves. This vine is a true sweet potato, and at the end of summer you can dig up the big tubers (which are edible but not considered tasty).

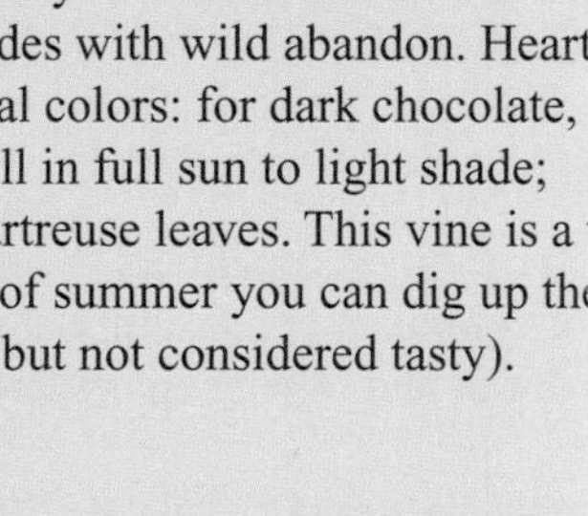

Mix and Match

Foliage and flowers mix it up to create a series of three stair-stepped containers. Colorful shade-loving foliage plants are perfect container plants.

Persian Shield

Coleus

Begonia

Hibiscus

- **A. 2 Persian Shield** (*Strobilanthes dyerianus*) Zones 10-11
- **B. 4 Coleus** (*Solenostemon scutellarioides*) Annual
- **C. 2 Begonia Rex** Zones 10-11, annual elsewhere
- **D. 3 Sweet Potato Vine** (*Ipomoea batatas* 'Marguerite') Zones 9-11, annual elsewhere
- **E. 1 Chinese Hibiscus** (*Hibiscus rosa-sinensis*) Zones 9-11, annual elsewhere

CONTAINER GARDENS:
PLANT THEM YOUR WAY

Flowers and Foliage

Create flower-filled containers to brighten your outdoor spaces. Match or complement patio furnishings or house paint color, or just choose flower and foliage colors that look good to you.

LEFT Perennials make excellent container companions: lamb's ears, sedum, ornamental grass and veronica.

BELOW You don't have to mix and match flowers—you can just pile on the blooms of one. This wagon holds two big containers of scaevola. And because it's on wheels, it can easily be moved to wherever you need a spot of color.

RIGHT Plant for the shade. This container features 'Iron Cross' begonia, 'Red Thread' alternanthera, 'Kiwi Fern' coleus, white impatiens, 'Blackie' sweet potato vine, 'Nico' plectranthus and 'Petite Licorice' licorice vine.

SUBTLE BEAUTY

Mix and match silver-, white- and burgundy-hued plants to create a quiet but elegant container.

SILVER ANNUALS

Deadnettle 'White Nancy'
Dichondra 'Silver Falls'
Dusty Miller
Eucalyptus 'Silverdrop'
Flowering Kale

BURGUNDY ANNUALS

Ornamental Millet 'Purple Majesty'
Coral Bells 'Purple Palace'
Purple Fountaingrass 'Rubrum'
Bugleweed 'Bronze Beauty'
Basil 'Purple Ruffles'

WHITE ANNUALS

Petunia (any white variety)
Fan Flower 'Whirlwind White'
Verbena 'Aztec White'
Sweet Alyssum

EASY DOES IT

Starting out with a good-quality soil mixture made especially for containers will ensure a summer of gorgeous flowers. Look for mixes with sphagnum peat moss because this will help hold moisture in the soil. You need to water your container plantings at least once a day in hot weather because they'll dry out quickly.

HOW TO PLANT A LUSH CONTAINER GARDEN

1. TAKE UP SPACE In the bottom of a big pot place a plastic grower's pot turned upside down. You'll use less potting soil.

2. ADD SOIL Use potting soil (not soil from your yard) that has moisture-holding organic material such as sphagnum peat moss.

3. REMOVE PLANTS Carefully slide plant out of its grower's pot. Pull apart the roots a bit on the bottom of the plant so it can take in water better. Plant each in the container per your design.

4. REPLACE SOIL Tuck soil around the plants. Water your container and add more soil if it settles too much.

"The front exterior of my house needs a floral facelift. What are my options?" —Isabel

Window Boxes: Flower-Filled Views

Whether you are admiring it from outside or indoors looking out, a flower-and-foliage-filled window box is a double-sided treat. And no matter what size yard you have, you always can have a window box. If you are looking for the most rewarding gardening experience, a window-box garden may be all you need. Window boxes instantly improve curb appeal, they never require weeding, and you don't have to bend down to plant them.

Think of a window box as a must-have accessory for the exterior of your home. Adding instant decorative appeal, a window box (and the flowers!) can match the color of your home or its trim, or you can add a new color scheme. The color and texture of a window-box planting also can temper the look of your home. For example, if your home is angular and square, a window box of frilly and trailing flowers softens the hard edges.

There are a wide range of window-box materials to choose from: painted wood, stained wood, easy-care resin and metal. Where you install your window box will dictate what kind of plants you add. North-facing window locations will need shade-loving plants. South-side window boxes get sun lovers.

Before you mount the planter to the wall, make sure it has drainage holes in the bottom; if not, drill several. When you secure the planter to the house, use 3½-inch deck or lag screws and try to hit studs when possible. Once it's in position, fill the box with potting soil or container mix. These soil formulations are lighter than the soil in your yard and have moisture-holding components that help keep the container soil moist and your plants' root systems well hydrated. Then add your plants!

Care is easy. Just remember to water your window box at least once a day in hot weather. Because this garden is raised several feet off the ground, the wind will dry out the soil faster than the soil in your garden. And a foliar feeding a couple of times during the summer will keep your plants in top shape.

Create curb appeal. Plant electric-blue lobelia and yellow and red begonias for a color burst that can be seen from the street.

Spring Fling

Summer Sensation

Autumn Color

Winter Windowscape

Window Boxes in Four Seasons

Sun or shade, you can have a window box that offers gorgeous options for flowers and foliage. This small-space garden allows you to change your view by replanting your window box every season.

Spring Fling

Peek out your window and see spring coming to life right before your eyes with an early-season window box. Plant cool-weather flowers that can stand bouts of colder temperatures such as violas, pansies and forced-flowering spring bulbs.

Summer Sensation

When the weather warms up, fill your window box with heat-loving annuals and perennials. Choose both trailing and upright varieties. This window box includes impatiens, Jacob's ladder, hosta, variegated ground ivy, sweet potato vine and upright fuchsia.

Autumn Color

Fall window boxes can overflow with the bounty of the season: colorful gourds, mini pumpkins and corn with the husks intact. Late-blooming mums and asters are available in garden centers. Use the frilly foliage of flowering kale to add instant color. This window box features ivy, trailing petunia, kale and mums.

Winter Windowscape

A winter window box looks great with a dusting of snow or a fringe of frost. Planting winter-hardy shrubs is a great way to green up for the holidays. Gilded ornaments and lighting make the window box lovely at night too. This window box is planted with three small boxwoods; in colder climates use small globe arborvitae. 'Aurea Golden Globe' is hardy to -30 degrees F.

WINDOW BOX
BULK UP WITH SMALL SHRUBS

Talk about instant impact! Plant several small shrubs and you'll have a lush and lavish window box. Use miniature versions of your favorite shrubs: deciduous, flowering and coniferous. If they start to outgrow their space, you always can dig them up and plant them in your yard. An all-green window box complements any home exterior and is an especially great option for formal and contemporary home architecture. This window box features the following plants: lithodora, juniper, burro's tail, Korean boxwood and agave.

WINDOW BOXES: PICK YOUR PALETTE

Plant your window boxes with the colors that look best against your home's exterior. Match plant flower hues to the paint color of your home to create a customized look.

RED AND HOT

A. ***Petunia* x *hybrida*** 'Easy Wave Red'
B. **Scarlet Sage** (*Salvia splendens* 'Picante Scarlet')
C. **Coleus** (*Solenostemon scutellarioides* 'Wizard Mix')
D. **Coleus** (*Solenostemon scutellarioides* 'Kong Scarlet')
E. **Zonal Geranium** (*Pelargonium x hortorum* 'Designer Dark Red')

YELLOW SUNSHINE

A. **Trailing Petunia** (*Calibrachoa* 'Million Bells Yellow')
B. **Marigold** (*Tagetes* 'Inca Yellow')
C. **Gloriosa Daisy** (*Rudbeckia hirta* 'Irish Eyes')
D. **Shrub Verbena** (*Lantana camara* 'New Gold')
E. **Chrysanthemum** 'Fortune'
F. **Lollipop Plant** (*Pachystachys lutea*)

IN THE PINK

A. ***Zinnia elegans***
B. ***Diascia*** 'Lavender Pink'
C. **Rock Garden Pink** (*Dianthus* 'Little Jock')
D. **Egyptian Star Cluster** (*Pentas lanceolata* 'Butterfly Deep Pink')
E. **Transvaal Daisy** (*Gerbera jamesonii*)
F. **Flowering Tobacco** (*Nicotiana alata*)
G. **Ivy Geranium** (*Pelargonium peltatum*)

BLUES FEST

A. **Petunia** (*Petunia x hybrida* 'Suncatcher Sapphire')
B. **Cup Flower** (*Nierembergia* 'Purple Robe')
C. ***Nemesia*** 'Bluebird'
D. **Anise-Scented Sage** (*Salvia guaranitica* 'Black and Blue')
E. **Summer Snapdragon** (*Angelonia angustifolia* 'Angel Mist Lavender')

"I love fresh vegetables, and nothing beats the feeling of growing them myself." —Sally

Vegetable Gardens: Plant Great Tastes

Never has the prospect of growing your own food been so enticing—fresh lettuce plucked right out of the garden and served in a salad moments later; glistening strawberries for your morning cereal; baby potatoes eaten just moments after they've been unearthed. This is eating fresh!

Vegetable gardens can produce a wide variety of interesting foods—and things that are pricey or impossible to find in the grocery store. Leafy French greens, succulent baby carrots and glistening heirloom tomatoes—foods you find on the menus of exclusive restaurants—are easy to grow and satisfying to serve and eat.

Vegetable gardening allows you to taste the best of every season. In early spring you can sow cold-tolerant leafy vegetables such as lettuce, spinach and Swiss chard. Root crops, such as carrots, radishes and beets, as well as kale, Brussels sprouts, cauliflower and broccoli, also grow in cool weather. As early as March and April (depending on your growing zone) you can plant seeds and seedlings in your vegetable garden. You can harvest greens and radishes, planted from seed, in as little as 30 days. Each variety has its own maturity date, so check the seed packets to see when the vegetables you are planting will be ready.

As your spring crops grow, you can start to plan your summer vegetable garden. Hot-weather plants, such as tomatoes and peppers, can be set into the ground as seedlings as soon as the threat of frost in your area has passed. And while you dine on the delicacies of your summer garden, you can set in seedlings for a fall harvest. Some cool-weather plants, such as kale, can be harvested even after it has snowed.

From early spring to late fall, even a small raised-bed vegetable garden provides something fresh and tasty for your table.

Growing in Early Spring, Late Fall

You can fool Mother Nature by protecting your vegetable crops on either end of summer. Early spring and late fall vegetable growing is possible with a variety of gardening supplies that help keep small plants from getting too cold. There are many options, but they all provide the same thing—protection from the elements.

LEFT A garden cloche safeguards a tender seedling on a cold night.

BOTTOM LEFT Crop covers can stop plants from getting frostbite when the temperature dips.

BOTTOM RIGHT You don't have to spend a lot of money for plant protectors. Just cut off the bottom of a milk jug and slip it over the top of a tender seedling.

OPPOSITE A collar of water-filled tubes keeps the plant inside shielded from chilling temperatures.

The Taste of Summer

Nothing tastes like summer more than a fresh-picked sun-warmed tomato from your own backyard. Heirloom tomatoes allow you to taste the past as well. You won't find many of these old-world varieties in the grocery store, which makes them taste all the sweeter. What makes a plant an heirloom? There is more than one definition. One school of thought dictates that an heirloom variety must be at least 100 years old. Another uses the end of World War II (1945) as the date growers began to sell hybrid varieties. Regardless of the date, heirlooms represent a wide range of sizes, colors and tastes for tomato fans. Growing tomatoes at home may be the only way for you to taste some of these amazing, almost forgotten varieties.

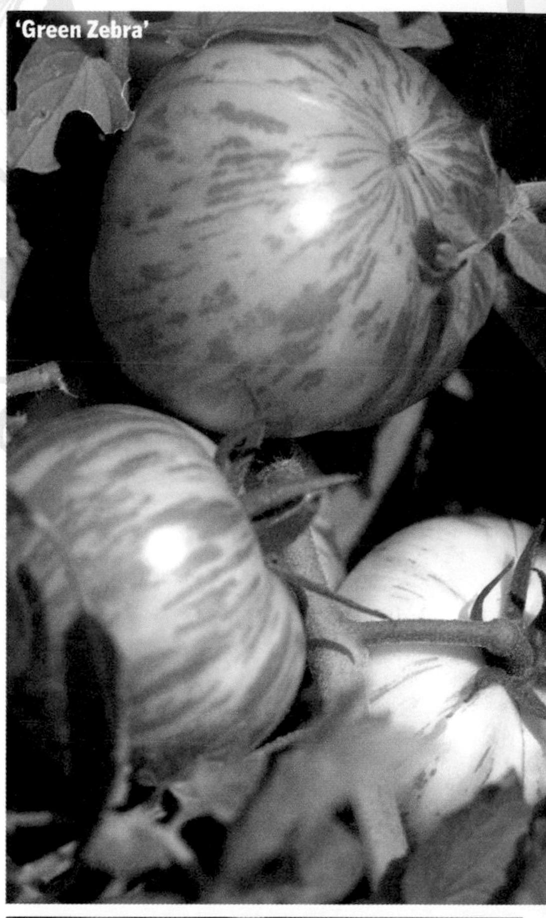
'Green Zebra'

'Black Cherry'

'Yellow Pear'

Assorted Heirloom Tomatoes

Square-Foot Garden

A 4×4-foot raised-bed garden looks as good as it tastes when you combine frilly kale, flowering chives, loose-leaf lettuce and sweet alyssum flowers to dress it up all season.

Kale | Chives | Lettuce | Sweet Alyssum

A. **7 Kale** *(Brassica oleracea)* Annual
B. **4 Chives** *(Allium schoenoprasum)* Zones 3–9
C. **12 Lettuce** *(Lactuca sativa)* Annual
D. **6 Sweet Alyssum** *(Lobularia maritima)* Annual

PLANT PROFILE
SWISS CHARD

THE LONGEST-LASTING GREEN

If you love loose-leaf greens but hate that the hot weather makes them bolt (flower and set seed) and turn bitter, you should add Swiss chard (*Beta vulgaris*) to your garden. Chard belongs to the beet family and withstands hot weather, providing greens for your table even at the height of summer. You can eat the dark-green leaves as well as the stalk, which comes in a variety of colors such as white, red and yellow.

A vegetable bed interplanted with flowers is attractive enough to have in your front yard.

Tomatoes are the most popular homegrown crop. You'll want to grow a lot—and many different types. Freeze them whole or make spaghetti sauce or salsa and enjoy fresh garden flavor all winter. Pick fruits when they are firm, full size and fully colored.

HOW TO GROW TERRIFIC TOMATOES

1. PLANT SEEDLINGS Choose healthy plants with good root balls. Tomatoes take 55 to 85 days to reach maturity, so planting seedlings is the fastest way to grow them.

2. MAKE THEM BUSHY Pinching off suckers (stems that grow up at the base of the main stem) makes plants bushier.

3. SET OUT CAGES Tomatoes need supports or cages to keep fruits off the ground and avoid pests and disease.

4. TIE THEM UP As plants grow, tie long tendrils to supports.

5. WEED OUT Keep the area around the base of your tomato plants free of weeds.

6. WATCH FOR PESTS Tomato hornworms are voracious leaf eaters. Look for them on the leaves and simply pluck them off and into a cup of soapy water.

The Beauty and Ease of Lettuce

Loose-leaf lettuce greens, arugula and spinach are all easy to grow from seed and quite prolific. They grow well in cool weather and take off once the temperatures rise. Cut often to keep plants from bolting (flowering and setting seed) once the weather warms.

HOW TO START VEGETABLE SEEDS

1. ASSEMBLE YOUR SUPPLIES You need seeds, a seed flat and growing mix.

2. ADD GROWING MIX. Fill all the holes in the seed flat.

3. MAKE SEED HOLES Use a pencil or stick. A small indentation is all that's needed.

4. PLANT SEEDS Use a seed planter or do it by hand. Lettuce seeds are extremely small.

5. WATER THE SEEDS Keep the growing mix moist but not soggy. Lettuce plants will sprout in several days.

6. START YOUR FAVORITES You can start multiple vegetables and herbs from seed.

EASY DOES IT
Heat-tolerant loose-leaf lettuces do well in containers on a patio. To extend the harvest, place containers where they receive a bit of afternoon shade.

"The sound of moving water is so soothing. I could sit out by my water garden all day." —Justine

Water Gardens: Go With the Flow

The lovely liquid burbling of a water garden is the sound of relaxation. Whether you install an inground pond or an aboveground water garden on your patio, water brings color, wildlife and soothing sound to your backyard.

Water gardening allows you to raise plants and flowers that don't exist in any other type of garden—those that grow in water, on water and at water's edge. You can enjoy exotic flowers such as water lilies, whose flat, dinner-plate-size leaves float languidly on the water's surface while stems topped with buds rise like snakes from below the water. Floating plants, such as water lettuce or water hyacinth, dot the surface of the water and provide shade and shelter to fish below. And there are a whole host of plants that love to sink their roots into the soggy soil that exists at the water's edge, among them yellow flag iris and frilly-topped papyrus.

Water gardens are also a magnet for wildlife. Toads and frogs will find your garden and make themselves right at home. You can add goldfish or koi (Japanese carp) which will spend hours swimming slowly through the water, their bright scales shimmering in the sun. (They also help keep the water clear and gobble up potential pests such as mosquito larvae.) Songbirds will visit your yard more often if there is a water source, and you may find these winged beauties dipping in for a bath or a drink. And beautiful insects such as butterflies and dragonflies will gravitate to the open water in your yard.

While water's reflective qualities make a water garden a calm and soothing place, the music sounds from water are prime reasons to install a water garden in your yard. Water tumbling over rocks or shooting out of a fountain adds natural sound to your backyard that you can enjoy both indoors and out.

LEFT Submerged water lilies and floating water lettuce create a dappled surface below which koi slowly swim.

RIGHT A watertight container inserted into a wooden whiskey barrel makes a perfect small-space water garden.

Lungwort

Spiderwort

Fringed Bleeding Heart

Deadnettle

Water Garden Oasis

A water garden uses a variety of different types of plants: edging (planted in the soil around the garden), marginal (planted in the wet soil that borders the water), floating (on the water surface) and submerged (planted in soil that is entirely underwater).

- **A.** **3 Lamb's-Ears** *(Stachys byzantina* 'Silver Carpet') Zones 4-8
- **B.** **1 Speedwell** *(Veronica spicata* 'Icicle') Zones 3-8
- **C.** **4 Azalea** *(Rhododendron)* Zones 6-8
- **D.** **3 Spiderwort** (*Tradescantia* spp.) Zones 5-9
- **E.** **1 Cranesbill** (*Geranium* spp.) Zones 5-9
- **F.** **3 Lady's Mantle** *(Alchemilla mollis)* Zones 4-7
- **G.** **4 Moss Pink** *(Phlox subulata)* Zones 3-8
- **H.** **3 Japanese Painted Fern** *(Athyrium niponicum* 'Pictum') Zones 5-8
- **I.** **3 Impatiens** (New Guinea Group) Annual
- **J.** **1 Fringed Bleeding Heart** *(Dicentra eximia)* Zones 4-8
- **K.** **4 Lungwort** *(Pulmonaria saccharata)* Zones 4-8
- **L.** **4 Variegated Japanese Sedge** *(Carex morrowii)* Zones 5-9
- **M.** **1 Ladybells** *(Adenophora confusa)* Zones 3-8
- **N.** **3 each of Japanese Iris** *(Iris ensata)* Zones 5-8 and **Siberian Iris** *(Iris sibirica)* Zones 4-9
- **O.** **4 Ribbongrass** *(Phalaris arundinacea)* Zones 4-9
- **P.** **3 Wood Fern** *(Dryopteris)* Zones 8-10
- **Q.** **10 Deadnettle** *(Lamium maculatum* 'White Nancy') Zones 4-8
- **R.** **6 Creeping Lilyturf** *(Liriope muscari* 'Silver Dragon') Zones 5-10
- **S.** **1 Hosta** (*Hosta sieboldiana* 'Elegans') Zones 3-8
- **T.** **6 Astilbe** (*Astilbe* 'Bridal Veil') Zones 4-9
- **U.** **1 Clematis** (*Clematis heracleifolia* var. *davidiana)* Zones 3-8
- **V.** **6 Pansy** *(Viola x wittrockiana)* Zones 4-8
- **W.** **1 Licorice Plant** *(Helichrysum petiolare)* Annual
- **X.** **1 Artemisia** (*Artemisia versicolor)* Zones 6-10
- **Y.** **3 Catmint** *(Nepeta* 'Six Hills Giant') Zones 4-8
- **Z.** **2 Water Lilies** (choice of hardy or tender)

PLANT PROFILE
WATER IRIS

SOME LIKE IT BOGGY

Yellow flag iris (*Iris pseudacorus*) is a popular and easy-to-grow bog plant that you can site at the edge of a water garden or directly in the water itself. Plants feature straplike green foliage and sunny-yellow flowers and can grow to 5 feet in height. The plant can spread, so it's important that you keep it contained in your own water garden and not allow it to escape into natural waterways where it can be a noxious weed. Pair it with cattails, another tall-growing bog plant.

A backyard water garden lures wildlife such as frogs, toads and waterfowl.

DO IT FOR LESS

Don't get sticker shock over the cost of installing a large garden. Instead "amortize" the cost by doing it over a series of years. For example, install a water garden one summer, plant shrubs and trees (and cost-saving annuals) the next summer, and fill in with perennials the following year.

Water Nymphs

The flower that inspired more than 250 oil paintings by French Impressionist painter Claude Monet, water lilies are the big event in a water garden. There are both hardy and tropical water lilies. Hardy water lilies can be left in the pond garden over the winter in cold climates. (If the pond freezes solid, you should bring your water lily in for the winter.) Tropicals are pickier about temperature and can't withstand a freeze. But both offer lovely, spiky blooms that rise magically out of the water. There are also day- and night-blooming varieties that allow you to enjoy the blooms whenever you are most often in your garden. Generally water lilies require a sunny location and still water to thrive. There are varieties that fit any water garden, from large and spreading to small and compact, the perfect size for a container garden.

'Chromatella' Water Lily

Hardy Water Lily

Tropical Water Lily

Hardy Water Lily

'Arc en Ciel' Water Lily

Amazon Lily

DO IT FOR LESS

If you want fish in your water garden but don't want to spend the cash for koi, try goldfish. These inexpensive fish can be purchased at pet stores for as little as a dime each. They are hardy and will grow quickly but will not get as large as koi.

Dive into Water Gardening

One of the most exciting aspects of a water garden is stocking it with fish. And the most prized fish in the water garden are koi. Brilliant hues and distinct markings make these fish a water garden's animated jewels. You can buy koi from pet stores or garden centers. And there are many koi breeders who specialize in rare and unusual types. Koi can range in size from several inches to more than a foot long. Their price depends on their size and coloring. You can pick up a small koi for a couple of bucks or you can spend thousands of dollars for large, exotic varieties.

HOW TO POT UP A HARDY WATER LILY

1. REMOVE WATER LILY Take it out of the packaging and separate roots and leaves. Remove any dead leaves.

2. FILL PLANTING BOX Use heavy soil (not potting soil) and gravel to create a planting base for the water lily. Use a container that is 12 to 18 inches wide and 6 to 10 inches deep.

3. PLACE LILY Plant the tuber close to the edge of the planting box and carefully spread the roots out in the container.

4. FILL CONTAINER Use just enough soil and gravel to bury the water lily roots.

5. ADD GRAVEL Fill to the top of the container to keep the soil from leaching out into the pond water.

6. SET IN WATER Place the water lily into the water garden or pond so that it is submerged 12 to 18 inches under water. If your pond is deeper than that, place the container on bricks to bring it to the correct level.

"My yard is like a postage stamp, so my garden has to be compact. But I also want lots of color." —Ellie

Small-Space Gardens: Tiny But Beautiful

Whether you have a tiny yard—or a large yard in need of color infusion—small-space gardening is a way to brighten the areas around your home. Many specialty gardens such as rock gardens, knot gardens and parterres take very little space to make a big impact.

Look for underused areas in your yard that a small garden can brighten up. You might be surprised that you can plant a gorgeous garden in a narrow strip of soil between your home's foundation and a walkway. Or decorate the ground around the base of your mailbox—it's a garden view you'll admire every day when you collect your mail. You can even reclaim the area in your front yard between your sidewalk and street that is usually relegated to a boring strip of lawn.

An added benefit of small gardens is they don't take much time to plant or maintain. And they are usually an inexpensive way to dress up underused and unnoticed areas in your yard. To keep garden maintenance as carefree as possible, group plants in your small gardens that have similar growing requirements; they'll all have the same needs for sunlight and moisture.

To save money, sow annual seeds right in the ground and enjoy a patch of a single flower in a single color. Or sow several seed packs of different annuals to create a tiny flower meadow. The easiest seeds to start directly in the ground include aster, cosmos, flowering tobacco, marigold, moonflower, poppy, snapdragon, sunflower and zinnia.

Shop for small versions of bigger plants for small-space gardens. Many species of perennials, shrubs and trees feature varieties that grow in compact or dwarf forms. You can also take advantage of vertical space by training flowering annual vines, which take up little ground space, on a trellis. Or look for tall shrubs, such as columnar versions of yew, arborvitae and other hedging shrubs, to grow up instead of out.

Small gardens can pack in a lot of color when you plant perennials and annuals in masses. This garden features color blocks of pink coneflower, orange marigolds, white dusty miller and yellow heliopsis.

Dwarf Fountain Grass
Dwarf Korean Lilac
Dwarf Alberta Spruce
Catmint

SIZED FOR SMALL SPACES

When garden space is at a premium, choose mini versions of the plants you love. These Tiny Tims look great in small spots and don't take up the space of their larger siblings. You can find dwarf versions of annuals, perennials, trees and shrubs.

Dwarf Fountain Grass

Grasses can overwhelm a small area, but there are compact growers such as *Pennisetum alopecuroides* 'Hameln.' This 2-foot-tall clump-forming fountain grass features arching bright-green stems topped with wheat-colored tassels. Dwarf fountain grass tolerates full sun to light shade. Zones 5 to 9.

Dwarf Korean Lilac

If you love lilacs but don't have the space for the large, old-fashioned types, try a scaled-down version. For small flower borders and even containers, dwarf Korean lilacs (*Syringa meyeri*) offer all the charms of the larger versions: sprays of pink or lilac blooms and a rich, intoxicating scent. 'Palibin' is a small variety that grows 4 to 6 feet tall. Zones 4 to 7.

Dwarf Alberta Spruce

Dwarf Alberta spruce (*Picea glauca*) has a compact, conical shape that is perfect for small gardens. This slow-growing spruce reaches 20 feet at maturity—but is much smaller compared with other spruces that can reach 70 feet tall. 'Conica' offers dark-green foliage all year round and maintains its compact, conical shape without pruning. New spring growth is lime green. Zones 3 to 6.

Catmint

An easy-to-grow perennial, catmint (*Nepeta racemosa*) produces mounds of gray-green foliage topped with delicate, lilac-blue flowers. This drought-tolerant and deer-resistant plant blooms from June until after frost. Catmint prefers well-drained soil and full sun to partial shaded locations. To promote continued bloom all summer, shear off the flower spikes after first flowering. Choose low-growing varieties, such as 'Little Titch,' for small-space gardens. Zones 3 to 9.

EASY KEEPERS

If your small-space garden includes the area around the foundation of your house, you may find the soil less than perfect. Often the topsoil is removed during home construction, so there may be an abundance of clay and very little soil. Till in nutrient-rich compost to help break up clay particles. You also can choose perennials that excel in clay soil with little or no help. Here are a few options:

ASTILBE
Shade-loving astilbe produces feathery spires of bloom.

MONARDA
Also called bee balm, flowers offer fringed blooms that attract butterflies.

VERBENA BONARIENSIS
Purple flowers top long waving stems.

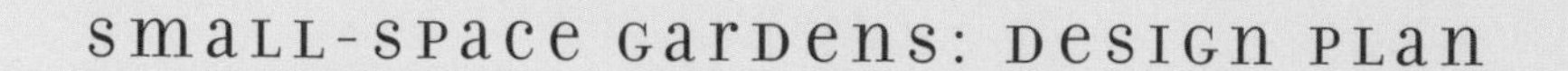

Sizzling Side Yard

Get the most out of cramped space by planting a strip of colorful annuals and perennials. This shady side yard features the lush Christmas fern, a great choice because it keeps its green color nearly all year.

Columbine

Tuberous Begonia

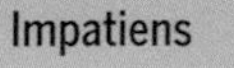

Impatiens

Fern

- **A.** **3 Christmas Fern** *(Polystichum acrostichoides)* Zones 3-8
- **B.** **2 Tuberous Begonia** *(Begonia x tuberhybrida)* Zones 9-10
- **C.** **11 Red and Pink Impatiens** (*Impatiens walleriana*) Annual
- **D.** **6 Wishbone Flower** *(Torenia fournieri)*, Annual
- **E.** **2 Columbine** *(Aquilegia x hybrida)* Zones 3-9

PLANT PROFILE
TORENIA

COLOR FOR SHADY SPOTS

An easy going shade annual, torenia is also called wishbone flower and clown flower because of its vividly colored flowers. A colorful choice for shady spots, torenia grows easily from seed sown indoors in pots or outdoors in the ground.

Use colorful annuals and perennials to brighten up a narrow walkway.

Serenity Fountain Garden

You don't need a big space to create a little pocket of serenity in your yard. And nothing soothes the senses more than a combination of beautiful blooms and the sound of flowing water.

A water feature, even a small one, transforms a small garden into an eye-catching oasis.

A. **3 Impatiens** (*Impatiens walleriana*) Annual
B. **3 European Wild Ginger** (*Asarum europaeum*) Zones 4-
C. **2 Big Blue Lilyturf** (*Liriope muscari*) Zones 5-10
D. **1 Kangaroo Paw** (*Anigozanthos*) Zones 9-10
E. **1 Coleus** (*Solenostemon scutellarioides*) Annual
F. **1 Hummingbird's Mint** (*Agastache cana*) Zones 5-10

HOW TO MAKE A BUBBLING FOUNTAIN

1. CUT THE LINER Fit and place it in the bowl. It should be slightly higher than the top of the bowl. Avoid trimming excess until the fountain is assembled because the gravel and water will pull the liner down.

2. INSERT THE SAUCER Place it upside down on the liner in the bottom of the bowl. Make sure the pump fits under the saucer with the liner in place. Remove the saucer and drill several drainage holes, a hole in the center for the plastic tubing and one on an edge for the pump cord. (Make sure to wear protective eyewear.)

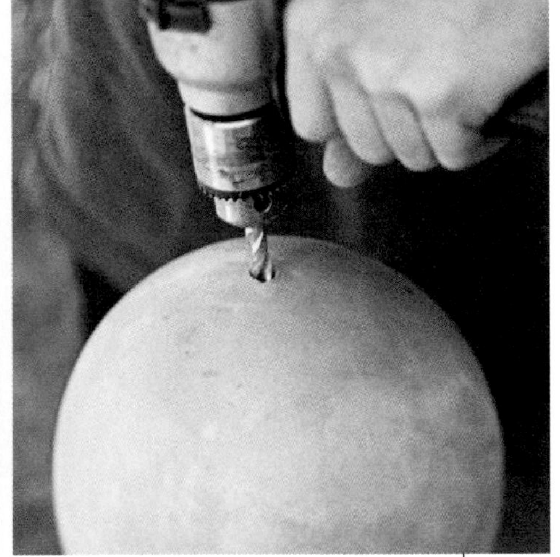

3. DRILL A HOLE Drill in the top center of the sphere. Use a drill bit slightly larger than the diameter of the plastic tubing.

EASY DOES IT

Get the right size pump. Pumps are sized by gallons-per-hour (GPH) output. For a fountain this size, buy a submersible pump capable of pumping 60-80 gallons per hour.

4. INSERT TUBING Place the saucer upside down, then feed the tubing through the hole in the sphere.

5. CENTER THE SPHERE Connect the tubing from the saucer to the pump outlet and set the sphere back in the bowl. Gently tug on the tubing so it runs straight up from the pump, through the saucer and out the top of the sphere. Fill the bowl with water and plug in the unit to test.

6. ADJUST LINER Make sure it is evenly distributed throughout the bowl. There should be no low spots in any of the folds. Trim excess. Add pebbles on top.

Flower Tower Garden

Rise to new heights! Take advantage of vertical growing options when you're short on ground space. A wooden trellis against a wall or freestanding wrought-iron obelisk offers climbing vines a leg up.

Angels' Trumpets

Black-Eyed Susan Vine

Cockscomb

Daylily

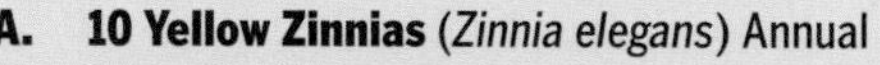

- **A. 10 Yellow Zinnias** (*Zinnia elegans*) Annual
- **B. 1 Angels' Trumpets** (*Brugmansia* spp.) Zones 10-12
- **C. 1 Black-Eyed Susan Vine** (*Thunbergia alata*) Zones 9-10, annual elsewhere
- **D. 2 Yellow Cockscomb** (*Celosia* spp.) Annual
- **E. 2 Yellow Daylily** (*Hemerocallis* spp.) Zones 3-10

Build a garden bed around a color scheme. Yellow and orange plants offer a bright "hello" in an entryway garden.

small-space gardens: design plan

Mailbox Makeover

Beautify your mailbox by planting a garden around it—or build your garden around a lamppost or a flagpole. This island garden makes a fantastic focal point.

A. **1 Verbena** (*Verbena* x *hybrida*) Zones 9-11, annual elsewhere
B. **2 Purple Wave Petunia** (*Petunia* x *hybrida*) Annual
C. **1 Dahlberg Daisy** (*Dyssodia tenuiloba*) Annual
D. **2 Impatiens** (*Impatiens walleriana*) Annual
E. **4 Sweet Alyssum** (*Lobularia maritima*) Zones 10-11, annual elsewhere
F. **3 Dusty Miller** (*Centaurea cineraria* 'Silver Dust') Zones 7-11
G. **1 Clematis** (*Clematis* 'Ville de Lyon') Zones 4-9
H. **1 Dahlia** (*Dahlia* x *hybrida*) Annual
I. **2 China Pink** (*Dianthus chinensis*) Annual
J. **3 Globe Amaranth** (*Gomphrena globosa*) Zones 9-11, annual elsewhere
K. **3 Geranium** (*Pelargonium* x *hortorum*) Annual

Dahlberg Daisy

China Pink

Dahlia

Purple Wave Petunia

Even the smallest gardens have big impacts when you use attractive focal points and colorful vertical accents.

PLANT PROFILE

CLEMATIS 'VILLE DE LYON'

SOCIAL CLIMBER

A profuse bloomer in late spring and early summer, *Clematis* 'Ville de Lyon' also may flower again in late summer. It's beautiful growing up a post or on a wooden fence or an arbor. The rich garnet color is a standout—and the flowers are big enough to be noticed from far away.

Curbside Appeal

Install a colorful street-side garden that's filled with fuss-free flowers. Native plants are a wise choice for curbside plantings because they love nonstop sun and need little water beyond what Mother Nature provides.

'Fireworks' Goldenrod

Oxeye Daisy

Baptisia

Purple Coneflower

A. **6 Garden Phlox** (*Phlox paniculata* 'Shortwood') Zones 4-8

B. **4 Blue False Indigo** (*Baptisia australis*) Zones 3-9

C. **5 Switchgrass** (*Panicum virgatum* 'Northwind') Zones 3-9

D. **5 Purple Coneflower** (*Echinacea purpurea*) Zones 3-8

E. **3 Smooth Astar** (*Aster laevis* 'Bluebird') Zones 3-9

F. **4 Bee Balm** (*Monarda didyma* 'Jacob Cline') Zones 4-10

G. **4 New England Blazing Star** (*Liatris scariosa* var. *novae-angliae*) Zones 4-8

H. **4 Goldenrod** (*Solidago rugosa* 'Fireworks') Zones 3-9

I. **2 Oxeye Daisy** (*Heliopsis helianthoides* 'Summer Nights') Zones 3-9

J. **3 Turtlehead** (*Chelone glabra*) Zones 3-8

PLANT PROFILE
PHLOX

FRAGRANCE AND FLOWER

Phlox paniculata is commonly called garden or border phlox. Plants grow 3 to 4 feet tall and bear large trusses of fragrant flowers from summer to early fall. This old-fashioned favorite is easy to care for and very showy.

A street-side border of drought-tolerant perennials improves the curb appeal of your home and requires little care.

"I love the trees in our yard but I want a garden too. What plants can take low light levels?" —Amanda

Shade Gardens: Lush and Colorful

Shade gardens may look very "green" in large part due to their dependence on the types of foliage plants that thrive in areas of limited sun. A surprising number of plants grow well only in the shade. Low-growing woodland wildflowers, such as lungwort, forget-me-not and jack-in-the-pulpit, offer shade gardeners a wild mix of options. Leafy perennials including the versatile hosta, wild ginger and taro fill in shady spaces and never miss the lack of light. Shady spots also are excellent homes for fine-leaved understory trees such as Japanese maples and redbuds.

But don't let anyone tell you that you can't have color in your shade garden. Astilbes offer vibrant bloom spires in red, pink and white. Bugbane produces rocketlike white blooms. And coralbells, caladium and begonias add colorful leaves and flowers that lighten up the darkest spots.

All shade is not created equal. There is deep shade cast by large, leafed-out deciduous or coniferous trees. Sparsely leafed trees produce a dappled shade. Partial shade describes an area that is in shade for only part of the day. Then you get the best of both worlds: a shade-and-sun garden. To best plan your garden you need to study how the sun moves across it. Once you see what kind of light exists in your garden you can choose your flowering and foliage options.

A shade garden is a low-maintenance garden. It generally needs less weeding. If you mulch well and pack in leafy plants shoulder to shoulder, there will no place for weeds to elbow their way in. You may also need to water less because shady spots—not baked by the sun—are able to retain ground moisture longer.

If you're looking for a garden retreat, there's no better place than a shade garden. Its soothing plant palette, array of interesting textures and cooling shadows offer an ideal setting for a path leading to a bench, pergola or woodland gazebo.

SHADE GARDENS: DESIGN PLAN

Woodland's Edge Garden

The area that separates lawn from a group of large trees is the perfect spot for a shady border. Woodland gardens showcase the leafy talents of hostas and the bright airy colors of astilbe. Variegated foliage—leaves that are two-toned—adds extra light.

Black Mondograss

Hosta 'Frances Williams'

Astilbe

Ostrich Fern

- **A. 3 Black Mondograss** (*Ophiopogon planiscapus* 'Nigrescens') Zones 6-10
- **B. 1 Variegated Redtwig Dogwood** (*Cornus alba* 'Elegantissima') Zones 3-8
- **C. 1 Lily** (*Lilium* hybrids) Zones 3-9
- **D. 6 Astilbe** (*Astilbe* x *arendsii* 'Fanal') Zones 4-8
- **E. 1 Hosta** (*Hosta* 'Frances Williams') Zones 3-8
- **F. 1 Hosta** (*Hosta sieboldiana* 'Elegans') Zones 3-10
- **G. 1 Hosta** (*Hosta* 'Halcyon') Zones 3-10
- **H. 1 Ostrich Fern** (*Matteuccia struthiopteris*) Zones 2-9
- **I. 5 Impatiens** (*Impatiens walleriana*) Annual

IMPRESSIVE FOLIAGE

This is one big hosta. *Hosta sieboldiana* 'Elegans' grows 3 to 4 feet in diameter and features large leaves (10 to 13 inches across!) that are heart-shaped, corrugated and a lovely shade of blue-green. In the summer, this hosta is topped with gorgeous white flowers that are beautiful enough to cut for bouquets. It provides color, contrast, texture and bulk to a shaded bed or border. 'Elegans' is a slow grower, taking several years to reach its mature shape, but it is worth the wait. Another plus is that this hosta's dense foliage shades out the possibility of any weeds gaining a roothold around it. The plant likes well-drained soil and will flourish in partial to full shade.

Variegated dogwoods add light to shade gardens and feature showy red stems that look great all winter.

Wishbone Flower
Wax Begonia
Browallia
Scarlet Sage

Shade Gardens annuals

Turn on the lights in your shady garden with colorful annuals. Tuck them into woodland gardens or line them up on the shady side of your home and build a bed beneath a big shade tree.

Wishbone Flower

Wishbone flower or torenia (*Torenia fournieri*) is a relatively new choice for shade gardens. The flower, in a shape similar to a snapdragon, blooms in a range of bright colors such as purple and pink. Torenia grows easily from seed sown indoors in pots or outdoors in the ground. Plants grow 8 to 12 inches tall and bloom nonstop until frost.

Wax Begonia

A popular and reliable shade planting, wax begonias (*Begonia* x *semperflorens*) offer lots of different flower and leaf color choices. Oval glossy leaves are available in green, mahogany, bronze, red or variegated forms. The blooms of wax begonias can be single or double—in red, pink, rose and white. These tender perennials have succulent stems and, depending on the variety, bloom in attractive little mounds that range in size from 6 to 18 inches tall.

Browallia

Bearing beautiful small, blue flowers, browallia also is called amethyst flower or sapphire flower. A tidy mounding plant, browallia is a good choice for containers or planted as a border edging plant. It does best in rich soil high in organic matter, so add compost in the planting holes. Water well and mulch around the plants to keep soil cool and moist. Browallia likes the heat and may not bloom in summers that stay cool. Plants grow 1 to 2 feet tall.

Scarlet Sage

The spired blooms of this red salvia (*Salvia splendens*) will add a little sizzle to your shade border or container plantings. This native of Brazil blooms in a wide range of colors, including white, salmon or purple, plus the traditional bright red. Plants grow from 8 inches to nearly 3 feet tall. When flowers drop off, cut back the plant to encourage a second flowering.

PLANT PROFILE IMPATIENS

If you have a shady yard, you should get to know all the varieties of impatiens. Pack them into containers and window boxes, sprinkle them along the edges of woodland paths and mound them into beds. Impatiens bloom in just about every color except true blue. And if you have a bright spot inside, you may be able to grow them all year as an indoor plant.

'SUPER ELFIN WHITE' Illuminate shady spots with dazzling white flowers on compact 10-inch-tall plants.

'FIESTA PURPLE' DOUBLE IMPATIENS Get double the flowers! Rose-like flowers offer a vivid color display.

'PIXIE PINK BICOLOR' MINI-IMPATIENS Enjoy small, creamy-pink flowers splashed with darker pink on 12-inch-tall plants.

Hosta + Leatherleaf Fern

Leaves and Flowers

Creating an interesting shade border is easy when you pair textural plants such as ferns, hostas and lady's mantle. Large-leafed plants make a statement and offer lots of choices. Hostas range in leaf size from small to huge. If you are looking for extra large leaves, try 'Earth Angel' or 'T-Rex.' Caladium and taro also add an impressive amount of foliage to a sunless garden. Blooming perennials include astilbe, forget-me-nots, begonia, lungwort and primula.

Lady's Mantle + White Begonia

Red Astilbe + Pink Astilbe

Ostrich Fern + Japanese Maple

Lungwort + 'Georgia Peach' Coral Bells

'Halcyon' Hosta + Japanese Painted Fern

Caladium + Begonia + Polka-Dot Plant

Foliage-Filled Shade Border

Creating a garden based on foliage is an excellent way to enjoy multiseason color. This bed design plays up contrasting plant shapes, placing big leaves next to strappy ones, upright plants alongside weeping forms. This curving border grows in partial shade, so the darkest areas of the garden feature yellow and variegated foliage plants to brighten things up.

A. **2 Japanese Forest Grass** (*Hakonechloa macra* 'Aureola') Zones 5-9

B. **1 Winter Daphne** (*Daphne odora*) Zones 7-9

C. **2 Tree Peony** (*Paeonia suffruticosa*) Zones 4-9

D. **2 Mexican Orange Blossom** (*Choisya ternata*) Zones 8-10

E. **4 Brown-Eyed Susan** (*Rudbeckia triloba*) Zones 3-10

F. **3 Chocolate Snakeroot** (*Eupatorium rugosum* 'Chocolate') Zones 4-8

G. **4 Angelwing Begonia** (*Begonia coccinea*) Zones 9-11

H. **1 Rhododendron** (*Rhododendron* spp.) Zones 5-11

I. **1 Banana** (*Musa sikkimensis*) Zones 8-11

J. **1 Winter Heath** (*Erica carnea*) Zones 5-8

K. **7 Foetid Iris** (*Iris foetidissima*) Zones 6-9

L. **3 Japanese Anemone** (*Anemone x hybrida*) Zones 5-9

Japanese Anemone

Chocolate Snakeroot

Banana

Mexican Orange Blossom

PLANT PROFILE
HAKON GRASS

GRACEFUL IN THE SHADE

This elegant, sweeping grass is called Japanese forest grass and is one of the few ornamental grasses that thrive in shade. Mounding clumps of arching leaves gradually increase in size, but this plant never becomes invasive (as some grasses can). *Hakonechloa macra* 'Aureola' lightens shaded spots in the garden with its lovely golden-yellow leaves striped with green. Hakon grass does best in moisture-retaining humus-rich soil, but it will also tolerate dry conditions. Plants grow 12 to 14 inches tall and 12 to 16 inches wide.

The edge of a woodland garden may receive partial sunlight—so make use of it by tucking in sun-loving plants.

"My garden changes so much in every season. I can't wait to see what is blooming next." —Christina

Three Seasons: Three Borders

When you think about planting a garden, consider the seasons of bloom for each of the plants you select. To enjoy the color and the flowers outside your window from early spring until frost, you need to plant a wide variety—bulbs, perennials and annuals—to keep the color show going. Although many are long bloomers, there isn't really any plant that starts blooming in early spring and continues through to frost. That's why you have to create a choreograpy in your garden.

When you plan your garden, make a list of your favorite plants for each season. What are the spring-blooming bulbs and perennials you like best? What color schemes do you prefer for your summer garden? Then think of which perennials, annuals and bulbs bloom in those hues. And if you want to enjoy a final color burst at the end of the gardening season, select your favorite fall bloomers to add to the mix. Create a garden plan that uses all of these plants to ensure that you'll have color all through the growing season.

A garden isn't a static event—that's what makes it so exciting. Every day something new, albeit subtle, happens. Buds form, flowers open up, petals fall and litter a path like so much confetti. By planning for blooms in all seasons, from spring to fall, you can enjoy your garden at its best all the time.

Appreciate every nuance of your garden as it grows throughout the season. Take a walk through the beds and borders and enjoy the flowers, scents and beauty of the world in your own yard.

Fritillaria + Tulip

Spring Vignettes

Spring's warm weather brings a burst of bloom in the garden. Early-flowering bulbs, such as *Scilla siberica*, glory of the snow (*Chionodoxa*) and puschkinia spread and intermingle to create a bright carpet of bloom. Narcissus and tulips offer many early, mid- and late-spring blooming varieties—in so many different flower forms! You can choreograph their bloom times to coincide with early-blooming perennials such as bleeding heart, peony, lily-of-the-valley and hellebore. Allium, with its giant purple globed flowers, and *Fritillaria persica,* with its dark-purple spires of pendulous flowers, look stunning when paired with tulips, peonies or deciduous or evergreen shrubs.

Boxwood + Allium

Tulip + Hellebore

Tulip + Puschkinia

'Fancy Frills' Tulip + 'Queen of the Night' Tulip

Peony + Allium

Glory of the Snow + *Scilla siberica* 'Spring Beauty'

"Wake Up" Spring Bulb Garden

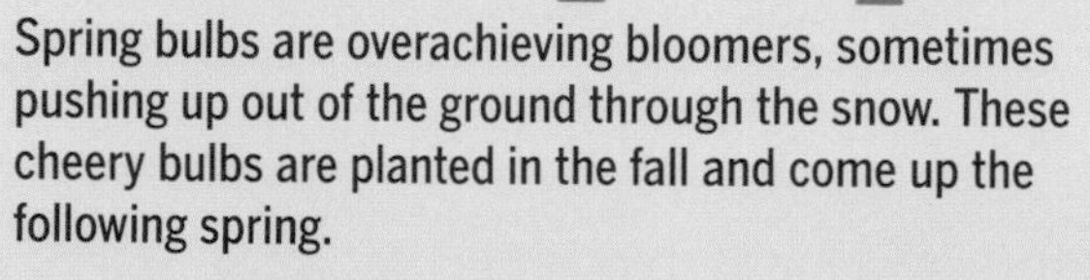
Spring bulbs are overachieving bloomers, sometimes pushing up out of the ground through the snow. These cheery bulbs are planted in the fall and come up the following spring.

A. **30 Hyacinth** (*Hyacinthus orientalis*) Zones 4-8
B. **50 Grape Hyacinth** (10 groups of 5 each) (*Muscari amerniacum*) Zones 3-8
C. **70 Yellow Daffodil** (14 groups of 5 each) (*Narcissus*) Zones 3-10
D. **40 Red Darwin Hybrid Tulip** (8 groups of 5 each) (*Tulipa*) Zones 4-8

Hyacinth

Grape Hyacinth

Narcissus

Tulip

PLANT PROFILE
DARWIN TULIPS

LONG-STEMMED BEAUTIES

The blossoms of Darwin tulips have a perfect pyramid shape when closed, but open out to flowers that can measure up to 6 inches across. A lovely cut flower, Darwins have long stems and bloom in gorgeous colors. Darwins return each year looking great—just make sure you allow the leaves to die back naturally in the spring. Don't remove them until they are totally dead; the bulbs use the leaves to gain the energy to bloom again the following year.

Bulbs look so natural in the landscape when you plant them in clusters. The cheery mounds of daffodils here each represent five bulbs per planting hole.

Double Impatiens + Dusty Miller

Summer Sizzle

Annuals and summer-blooming perennials make for amazing and colorful pairings in the garden, strutting their stuff in containers and window boxes. Go monochromatic and select one color theme by pairing pink 'Prairie Dawn' rose with 'Goldflame' honeysuckle or pink alyssum and fuchsia double petunias. Or create a parade of primary colors that march brightly through your garden with combinations of bright-yellow yarrow or heliopsis and red poppies or hollyhocks. Sometimes, ambitious growers devise a summer surprise of color such as the mingling of yellow-flowering variegated lantana and white petunias with just a hint of yellow at the throat.

'Prairie Dawn' Rose and 'Goldflame' Honeysuckle

Lantana + Licorice Vine + Petunia

Yarrow + Poppy

Petunia + Sweet Alyssum

Hollyhock + Oxeye Sunflower

Nicotiana + Dusty Miller

PLANT PROFILE
VERONICA

BLUE-SPIRED BLOOMS

Easy-to-grow veronica will never disappoint. This perennial comes in many forms. Some have mats with loose clusters of saucer-shaped flowers. Others feature erect spikes crowded with star-shaped or tubular flowers. Veronicas bloom in blue, purple, rosy pink and white. They like sunny locations and well-drained soil. Deadhead to extend bloom time. 'Sunny Border Blue' offers bright-blue flowers on 2-foot-tall stems.

Tall-blooming penstemon and Asiatic lilies take this summer border to new heights of bloom.

"Celebrate Color" Summer Border

Heat-loving plants sizzle into summer. Tightly planted perennials and summer bulbs (and lots of mulch!) keep this border weed-free.

Dahlia

Asiatic Lily

'Snowbank' Boltonia

Firecracker Penstemon

A. **12 Pink Dahlia Hybrids** (4 clusters of 3 each) Zones 8-11
B. **3 Red Dahlia Hybrids** (1 cluster of 3) Zones 8-11
C. **3 Spike Speedwell** (*Veronica* 'Sunny Border Blue') Zones 4-8
D. **3 Yellow Dahlia Hybrids** (1 cluster of 3) Zones 8-11
E. **10 Asiatic Lily** (2 clusters of 5 each) (*Lilium* 'Landini') Zones 4-8
F. **10 Asiatic Lily** (2 clusters of 5 each) (*Lilium* 'Sunny Crown') Zones 4-8
G. **2 Boltonia** (*Boltonia asteroides* 'Snowbank') Zones 4-9
H. **5 Firecracker Penstemon** (*Penstemon eatonii*) Zones 4-9
I. **3 Purple Moor Grass** (*Molinia caerulea*) Zones 4-9

Aster + Goldenrod

Flowering Kale + Dusty Miller + Chrysanthemum

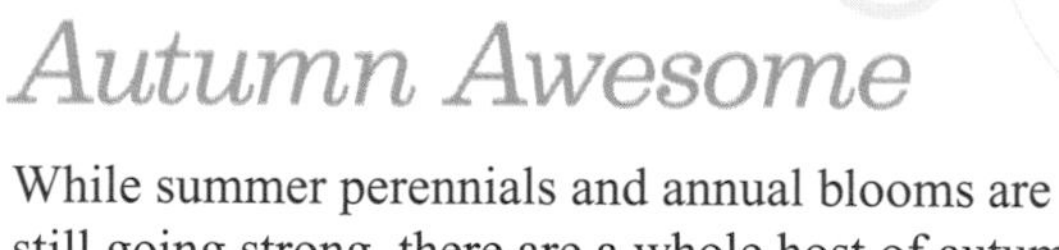

Autumn Awesome

While summer perennials and annual blooms are still going strong, there are a whole host of autumn bloomers that chime in for the swan song of the gardening season. Cool-season annuals, such as purple, yellow and white pansies and frilly-leafed ornamental kale rub shoulders with autumn-blooming perennials, including sunny goldenrod, snow-white boltonia and purple and pink asters. Late-season bulbs, among them, colchicum and autumn crocus, rise in a perennial border, peeking up beneath leaves of annuals. Plan for autumn color spectaculars by pairing late-summer blooming shrubs, such as hydrangea, with autumn-blooming chrysanthemums.

Hydrangea + Chrysanthemum

Purple Fall Crocus + White Colchicum

Pennisetum alopecuroides + Aster

Fall Colchicum + Lamb's Ears

'Janlim' Artemisia + 'Autumn Joy' Sedum

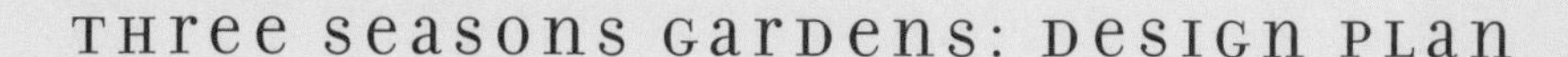
THREE SEASONS GARDENS: DESIGN PLAN

"Have a Fabulous Fall" Border

Autumn brings cooler weather and shorter days. But if you plan it right, your garden will continue to paint your landscape with blooms. Late-blooming perennials and bed edgers in the form of giant, colorful ornamental kale plants infuse this border with new life.

Flowering Kale

Silvergrass

Tickseed

'Autumn Joy' Sedum

- **A.** **3 Flowering Kale** (*Brassica oleracea*) Annual
- **B.** **5 Lady's Mantle** (*Alchemilla mollis*) Zones 4-7
- **C.** **3 Siberian Iris** (*Iris sibirica*) Zones 4-9
- **D.** **1 Bigleaf Hydrangea** (*Hydrangea macrophylla*) Zones 6-9
- **E.** **2 Silvergrass** (*Miscanthus sinensis*) Zones 4-9
- **F.** **5 Purple Coneflower** (*Echinacea purpurea*) Zones 4-9
- **G.** **3 Peony** (*Paeonia lactiflora*) Zones 2-8
- **H.** **4 Sedum** (*Sedum* 'Autumn Joy') Zones 3-9
- **I.** **4 Threadleaf Tickseed** (*Coreopsis verticillata* 'Moonbeam') Zones 4-9

PLANT PROFILE
LADY'S MANTLE

DIAMOND-STUDDED LEAVES

Alchemilla mollis, commonly called lady's mantle, blooms in the spring; its chartreuse flowers appear in frothy clusters above the foliage. The soft, flat leaves continue to look great in the garden throughout summer and into autumn. You'll love this plant after a rainy day or heavy dew—caught water droplets make each scalloped leaf look as if it is studded with diamonds. Use lady's mantle to soften the edge of a shaded path or to create a lush groundcover in dappled shade.

Feathery silvergrass adds height (and a little sway on breezy days) to autumn borders. After frost comes, this ornamental grass will continue to look great. It adds textural interest when cold weather sets in.

Chapter Five

PICKING THE RIGHT PLANTS

Grow fantastic flowers everywhere in your yard! It's easy when you know what plants need for success. Perennials, annuals, bulbs, shrubs and trees—find out how they can color your yard in every season.

CARE & MAINTENANCE
GUIDE & la CONSERVACION
LIGHT
Part Sun - Morning Sunlight Only
LUZ
Sol parcial - Solamente luz del sol mañanero
WATER USAGE
Semi-Moist
AGUA
Semi-húmedo
BLOOM TIME
Late Summer to Fall
TIEMPO DE FLORECER
Tarde en el verano a otoño
SPACING
10-12"
ESPACIAMENTO
25-30cm
GROWTH RATE
Fast
CRECIMIENTO
Rápido
AVERAGE SIZE
24" x 12"
TAMAÑO PROMEDIO
60cm x 30cm
COLD HARDINESS
0 to -10°F
ZONE 6
USDA Plant Hardiness Zone
-18 a -23°C
PRUNING
Cut back in late winter
PODA
FERTILIZATION
Spring and summer
FERTILIZACION
Primavera y verano
Needs mid-day shade where summertime temperatures linger above 95°F.
PLANTING STEPS
1. Dig hole 2 times width of pot.
2. Set top of root ball even with ground level.
3. Combine planting mix and soil. Fill to ground level and tamp.
4. Form water basin. Water to settle soil.
5. Add layer of mulch. Check often for water until established.
1. Cave hoyo doble ancho maceta.

CHOOSE PLANTS FOR YOUR YARD

If you want your plants—trees, shrubs and flowers—to thrive and excel, select those that match the conditions in your yard: light levels, soil types and hardiness zone (based on temperature and rainfall range throughout the year). Choose plants wisely, and they'll grow with vigor. That's why the first question you should ask before you buy is, "What are the needs for this plant?"

Let there be light. All plants have a preference for the kind of light they will grow best in. For example most annual plants like sun, although luckily for those of us who try to garden in shade, there are also annuals that prefer less light. It's the same with perennials, shrubs and trees. They all have their own light requirements. If you plant them accordingly, they will grow like mad. If you don't, they will underperform and may even die.

Create satisfying soil. There are plants that will excel in just about every soil condition. You can choose plants to fit the ground in which you are working or you can improve the quality of your soil to broaden your plant choices. Soil drainage (the degree to which it holds or drains away water), soil composition (clay, sandy) and soil fertility (pH and nutrients) all determine what you can grow. You can do a soil test (ask your local nursery for a kit) to help you figure out how to change your soil to accommodate a wider range of plants.

Get in the zone. Some plants can live through a cold winter. Other plants can't take a dry summer. To help gardeners choose the plants that will do best in their yards, the United States Department of Agriculture (USDA) created a plant hardiness zone system. Use these zones as a guide when buying plants. If you want a perennial or shrub or tree to survive and grow year after year, the plant must tolerate year-round conditions in your area. These conditions include the lowest and highest temperatures as well as the amount and distribution of rainfall. The USDA Hardiness Zone Map divides North America into 11 separate zones. Each zone is 10 degrees F warmer (or colder) in an average winter than the adjacent zone. (In some versions of the map, each zone is further divided into "a" and "b" regions.)

Make the most of microclimates. Not all areas in your yard are the same. Some spots may be cooler or warmer—these areas are called microclimates. For example, the south-facing side of a house or garage makes a warmer microclimate than the north-facing side of the same building. Once you're aware of the microclimates in your yard, you can capitalize on them.

Choose natives. Native plants are those that are indigenous to your area. If your home, say, is located in an area that used to be prairie, you can be sure that prairie natives, such as purple coneflower, will do well in your yard. Planting natives is a popular gardening trend. It makes sense to use plants in your yard that would naturally grow there—they have already adapted to the type of soil, temperature range and typical rainfall amounts found there. In other words, native plants will be right at home in your garden because, in a way, they were there before you were.

Read plant tags. When you buy plants from a nursery, garden center or mail-order source, they'll give you all the information you need to choose the plants that will grow in your yard. Plant tags generally feature soil, light and zone requirements. A zone map may appear on the plant tag, or the plant's zone range (for example, *Rudbeckia* can grow in zones 4 through 9) may be designated. (Check catalogs or Web sites for zone information, too.) At the very least, if you know what kind of light your garden receives and what zone you live in, you will be a smarter plant shopper.

"I love to see plants come up in my garden each spring. What comes back year after year?" —Debra

Perennials: Many Happy Returns

Perennials are plants that die back in the winter but come back the following spring. You plant them once, and they get bigger and better each year they return. In fact many perennials grow so well that at some point they need to be divided, which is a bonus because you get free plants.

Each perennial blooms at a specific time in the season. For example, some perennials flower in early spring, and you can count on them every year. Most perennials only bloom once during a season, although there are many early-blooming species that if cut back may bloom again later in the season.

Although weather fluctuations may delay or speed up blooming—an unseasonably warm spring may accelerate flowering time—you can rely on your perennials to flower at a specific time each year. For example, spring-flowering hellebores bloom around Easter. (In fact this plant's common name is Lenten rose.)

Perennials are so consistent and dependable, you can plan your garden around their arrival time. Create beautiful seasonal combinations with season-long blooms in an ever-changing tapestry of flower colors and leaf textures. And although perennial plants may initially cost more than annuals, they are cost-saving options in the long run.

A mix of flowering and foliage perennials makes a varied border. Ornamental grass and lamb's ears add foliar texture. Cosmos, dianthus and alliums infuse the border with hues of pink and purple.

Bleeding Heart

Virginia Bluebells

Iris

Dianthus

Perennials for Spring

The first flowers of spring are always welcome sights. Early-bird perennials break soil about the same time bulbs are blooming, which can make for some beautiful combinations.

Bleeding Heart

This lovely perennial produces mounds of finely cut green foliage and stems that drip with beautiful, heart-shaped flowers in April and May. Plants grow 2 to 3 feet tall. *Dicentra eximia* offers fringed foliage. Bleeding hearts like partial to full shade, so they are perfect for a woodland garden. Zones 3 to 9.

Virginia Bluebells

Lavender buds open to powder-blue flowers. *Mertensia virginica* grows 1 to 2 feet tall with light-green or gray-green leaves. They prefer light shade to partial sun and do best in moist, wooded areas with rich soil. They appear in spring, and the foliage dies back by midsummer. They spread out, so you'll enjoy bigger masses each year. Zones 3 to 9.

Iris

There are several early-blooming irises: dwarf iris (*Iris cristata*), Siberian iris (*Iris siberica*) and variegated iris (*Iris pallida*). The iris presents a flower with a very distinctive shape, one that influenced the fleur-de-lis design. Irises produce flowers in shades of lavender, purple, blue and white. Some also emit a lovely fragrance. Zones 3 to 10, depending on the variety.

Dianthus

Commonly called carnations or pinks, these little versions of the boutonniere-type flower are frilly and fragrant. They bloom in several colors, including lavender, red, pink and white, as well as some interesting bicolors. Dianthus grows in full sun to partial shade and reaches 6 to 12 inches tall, depending on the variety. It's great tucked amid stones in rock gardens or as a border edger. Zones 4 to 10.

PERENNIAL PROFILE
PEONY

Peonies are one of the easiest-to-grow and longest-lived perennials. Red peony shoots rise from the ground in the early spring to become 2- to 3-foot tall shrubs. The flowers bloom in a wide range of colors (red, pink, white, yellow, orange) and as forms (single, double and petal-packed varieties). Beloved for their fragrance, peonies make excellent long-lasting cut flowers. Grow in zones 2 to 10.

'LOIS E. KLEHM' Fuchsia petals surround a golden center.

'CORAL SUPREME' The cupped shape and soft pastel hue make it a garden favorite.

'KRINKLED WHITE' White crepe-paper petals encircle a bright yolk-yellow center.

Coreopsis

Yarrow

Coneflower

Black-Eyed Susan

Perennials for summer

Just as spring perennials and bulbs fade away, a blaze of summer flowers heats up the garden with renewed color. Planning all-summer bloom in your garden is easy because there are so many color palettes to choose from.

Coreopsis

Commonly called tickseed, this bright-yellow fringed flower greets you in the garden all summer. 'Sunray' features double flowers. *Coreopsis lanceolata* has daisylike flowers with orange centers. And 'Moonbeam,' which was named Perennial of the Year in 1992, features clusters of light-yellow, daisylike blooms and green, airy, fernlike foliage. Zones 4 to 9.

Yarrow

The distinctive flat flower heads and lovely lacy foliage make yarrow (*Achillea millefolium*) a favorite perennial. Yarrow prefers full sun and is very drought tolerant. It flowers in many colors, including white, yellow, red, pink and lavender. Yarrow also is a butterfly attractant. 'Moonshine' has sunny-yellow flowers and grows 18 inches tall. Zones 4 to 10.

Coneflower

A prairie native, this is an extremely hardy and drought-tolerant plant, with purple petals surrounding an orange center. *Echinacea purpurea* grows 2 to 4 feet tall and loves a sunny location. One of the most low-maintenance perennials, it attracts butterflies and birds. Zones 3 to 10.

Black-Eyed Susan

The sunny yellow blooms of black-eyed Susan (*Rudbeckia*) are one of the summer's favorite flowers. Hardy, robust and long-flowering, black-eyed Susan is also a great cut flower. It loves full sun and is a native prairie plant that attracts butterflies, bees and birds. It's also fairly deer-resistant. There are annual black-eyed Susans too, so be careful to select a perennial form. Zones 3 to 10.

PERENNIAL PROFILE
DAYLILY

Carefree and consistent, daylilies are the perfect solution for gardeners who want lots of color with no hassle. Daylily plants create mounds of straplike green leaves with lily-like trumpet blooms. Technically not a lily, this perennial is called *Hemerocallis* and offers varieties in a wide range of colors. Divide plants every third year and you'll have lots of daylilies for your garden and for edging paths. This versatile plant likes full sun but will grow in partially shaded areas as well. Grows in zones 3 to 10.

'BIG SMILE' Soft pink-yellow petals are edged with a bit of a frill.

'ENTRAPMENT' Burgundy blooms feature white accents and a yellow throat.

'ROOT BEER' Russet petals burst from a sunny-yellow center.

'Autumn Joy' Sedum

Chrysanthemum

Goldenrod

Joe Pye Weed

Perennials for autumn

Fall flowers add new color and excitement to your garden right before the season ends. In late August a whole host of perennials fire up with color.

'Autumn Joy' Sedum
Sedums come in a wide range of heights and colors. 'Autumn Joy' is one of the big ones, with dramatic flower heads that bud in summer (in a chartreuse cluster) and open up to a rosy-russet flower in autumn. 'Autumn Joy' grows 2 to 2.5 feet tall. Zones 3 to 9.

Chrysanthemum
A sun-loving perennial, chrysanthemum comes in several flower forms that range from single-petaled to petal-packed. With a wide-ranging color palette, they can be used anywhere in the garden. They bloom in white, yellow, gold, bronze, red, pink, purple and burgundy and grow 2 to 3 feet high. Zones 3 to 9.

Goldenrod
Solidago offers golden-yellow sprays of bloom and lots of flowering options to light up the autumn garden. 'Little Lemon' features soft-yellow blooms. The flowers of 'Fireworks' look like bursts of pyrotechnics. Although goldenrod has gotten a bad rap for causing hayfever, the blame actually goes to ragweed, a weed that blooms at the same time. Zones 4 to 9.

Joe Pye Weed
A favorite butterfly attractant, this wildflower *Eupatorium* 'Chocolate' also looks good in garden beds and borders. It blooms from July until frost. It's a tall plant, so place it in the back of the border; some varieties can reach 10 feet tall. 'Chocolate' grows 3 to 5 feet tall and features masses of white flowers on chocolate-colored stems. It likes moist, shady spots but will thrive in a sunny location if kept well watered. Zones 4 to 8.

PERENNIAL PROFILE
ASTER

Some of the showiest plants in the fall garden, asters grow on sturdy, woody stems and are topped with blossoms in pink, purple, white and lavender. To achieve better bloom and stem branching, the general rule is to pinch asters back until the Fourth of July and divide every three years. Butterflies love this plant. Zones 3 to 8.

NEW ENGLAND ASTER Fringed petals surround a yellow-orange center.

PINK ASTER A very showy aster that grows 3 feet tall.

'MÖNCH' Enjoy masses of powder-blue flowers.

HOW TO BUY: PERENNIALS

- Look for perennials that have strong, healthy stems and nice blooms.
- Look for plants free of spots on the leaves, which may indicate disease.
- Check the container and buy plants that don't have roots growing through the drainage holes or pushing out of the sides.

PERENNIALS BY SIZE

LOW-GROWING (6 TO 8 INCHES)
Ajuga
Vinca
Pachysandra
Lamium
Sedum

MEDIUM HEIGHT (1 TO 3 FEET)
Lamb's Ears
Coreopsis
Daylily
Catmint
Russian Sage

TALL (4 TO 5 FEET—AND TALLER)
Perennial Sunflower
Maiden Grass
Bear's Breeches
Foxglove
Goldenrod

TOP 5 MOST FRAGRANT PERENNIALS

Peony
Phlox
Dianthus
Lily-of-the-Valley
Lavender

Lily-of-the-Valley

HOW TO DIVIDE PERENNIALS

Most perennials form clumps as they grow. Older clumps can become too large, which results in fewer blooms. Some perennial clumps die out in the middle. Before this happens, divide the plants, making several plants from one. Think of it as free plants!

1. DIG IN Depending on the type of perennial you're dividing, you can either dig out a section of the plant or dig up the entire clump and break it into sections. Each section that you replant must have both root and shoot growth attached.

2. DIVIDE THE CLUMP Perennials that have strong root systems, such as many grasses, are difficult to pull apart by hand. Cutting them with a spade or handsaw may be necessary. Smaller perennials, such as asters, can be easily separated by pulling the divisions apart by hand or by using a knife or garden trowel.

3. AMEND THE SOIL Give your new plant a good feeding by mixing compost or well-composted manure into the soil you removed from the planting hole. Use the amended mix to backfill, and replant your division as quickly as possible. To ease the shock of transplanting, pinch back growth. Reducing the shoot on the top of the plants helps maintain a balance between how much water the damaged roots absorb and how much moisture the shoots emit.

4. SHOWER WITH WATER Keep the transplanted perennial well-watered for several weeks. Even drought-resistant perennials need extra moisture after transplant until they become established. Treat your divided perennial as you would a new plant in your garden, watering it as needed when the weather turns dry.

"I like to change the color scheme in my garden each year. This year I'm into blues..." —Nicole

Annuals: Amp Up with Color

No other group of plants packs the color punch that annuals deliver. Because they live only one season, annuals pour all their energy into making the best flowers possible. It's the way these plants have developed—an annual completes its life cycle in one year. The more flowers it pumps out, the more seed it will produce. While perennials come back year after year, annuals power up to bloom like crazy over the summer because they have just one season to grow, seed and reproduce for the following year. They start blooming in summer and don't quit until the frost in autumn.

Smart gardeners take advantage of annual flowers' overachieving ways. You can use annuals to experiment with color, texture or height in planting areas. Since annuals come in all colors, sizes and flower forms, you can create an all-blue garden one year, then switch to a red theme the following year.

Because annuals complete their full life cycle in one year—sprouting from a seed into a blooming plant, which then sets seed—it's important to deadhead them. The term "deadheading" refers to removing the dead head of a spent flower. On most annuals, removing the dead flowers keeps the plant producing blooms.

If you live in warm climate, some annuals, such as geranium and shrub verbena, may actually be perennials for you. Angels' trumpets and fuchsia are two tropical plants that are hardy in the warmest zones, but gardeners in areas that receive frost treat these plants as annuals.

Annuals can be planted in the garden by seed, which is the most inexpensive way of growing them. But if you want a lush garden right away, buy annual seedlings at a garden center or nursery. Look for plants that are short and stocky, with flower buds, not blossoms. Annuals are sold in many different sizes. Packs of multiple small plants may be economical if you have a large area to plant or need a lot of a specific type of plant. Small plants take longer to fill out in the garden, but ultimately yield the same colorful result as larger plants. Pots of annuals may cost more but they create a bigger impact in the garden.

Plant annuals once the chance of an overnight frost is safely past. Freezing temperatures, even for just a short amount of time, are deadly to annuals. Protect your investment and make sure you don't lose your spring garden to a nippy overnight temperature dip.

Sweeps of color: Planting waves of annuals means your garden will be in bloom right up to frost. Annuals are sometimes called bedding plants because they fill up beds and borders so nicely.

Lobelia

Bachelor's Buttons

Scaevola

Blue Salvia

COLORFUL ANNUALS: BLUE

Blue hues have a calming and cooling effect in the landscape. In window boxes, containers or garden beds, blue flowers look great alone or mixed with yellow, orange and chartreuse annuals.

Lobelia

Talk about eye-catching—you can see neon-blue annual lobelia (*Lobelia erinus*) from across your yard. There are few blue flowers that are more vivid. The mounding type, called edging lobelia, is the best choice for tucking amid rocks in a rock garden or as footlights when planted along pathways or in the fronts of beds. The cascading type presents a brilliant sapphire waterfall of blooms when planted in window boxes or pots. Annual lobelia prefer the cooler weather of spring and fall; they stop flowering during the heat of summer. Shear it back then and it'll rebloom in the autumn. Plant in full sun or partial shade. Lobelia grows one foot tall and spreads out about one foot.

Bachelor's Buttons

This old-fashioned favorite, *Centaurea cyanus* features clear blue flowers with frilly petals; flowers top 1- to 3-foot-tall stems. Bachelor's buttons is a willing mingler, reseeding itself freely throughout your garden. The blooms are great for cutting and drying. Bachelor's buttons grows best in sandy loam and tolerates low-moisture conditions. You can sow seeds directly in your garden after the last frost in your region. Space plants approximately 6 to 12 inches apart. After the first blooms fade, deadhead them to encourage a second flowering. If you want bachelor's buttons to reseed and sprout the next year, stop deadheading and allow the plant to go to seed.

Scaevola

A native of Australia, *Scaevola aemula* has won the hearts of American gardeners. Also called fan flower because the pretty blue flowers form a little fan, this sun-loving annual takes the hottest of summer days in stride without wilting. In the ground or cascading from hanging baskets, scaevola produces an abundance of lavender-blue or white blooms all summer. Grows 4 to 9 inches tall and spreads out to 18 inches.

Blue Salvia

Used as a bedding plant, annual blue salvia (*Salvia farinacea*) creates a pool of cool blue in the garden when planted en masse. 'Victoria Blue' is a popular variety that grows 18 to 24 inches tall with long spires of true-blue flowers. This plant requires little care, is drought tolerant and has the added bonus of attracting hummingbirds and butterflies.

ANNUAL PROFILE
MILLION BELLS

Million bells is a great descriptor for the less-easy-to-pronounce *Calibrachoa*. This overachieving petunia look-alike is bright and versatile, grows quickly and flowers endlessly. Perfect for containers or hanging baskets because of its spilling-over-the-sides growth habit, million bells also can be tucked into the front of a border. There it will spread with wild abandon, which saves you money because you don't have to plant so many edging plants. Give it ample water—especially when planted in window boxes and containers—and feed several times during the summer. You'll be rewarded with a bounty of blooms.

'PURPLE' Planted with sweet potato vine, million bells cascades with abandon.

'TEQUILA SUNRISE' A russet-orange flower sparkles with tinges of yellow.

'LAVENDER' Light purple petals are etched with dark purple accents.

Snapdragon

Zinnia

Vinca

Globe Amaranth

COLORFUL ANNUALS: RED

Sizzling-hot red hues spice up gardens and containers. Crimson-flowering annuals come in a wide range of flower forms and sizes.

Snapdragon

If you want to make kids wide-eyed, show them a snapdragon (*Antirrhinum majus*). This "mouthy" plant gets it name from the fact that you can gently squeeze the sides of the intricately shaped flower and see "dragon's jaws" open and close. In the garden this showy plant stands tall—1 to 4 feet—with attention-grabbing spires of blooms. Snapdragons are cool-season annuals that add color to fall borders too. Plant snapdragon in early spring, a few weeks before your last frost date. Remove the spent blooms to encourage more flowering. Snapdragons will self-seed in the landscape if not deadheaded. 'Red Rocket' blooms in red. Snapdragons also flower in pink, yellow, orange and white.

Zinnia

One of the easiest to grow and most colorful annuals (not to mention great cutting flowers), zinnias (*Zinnia*) won't disappoint. They grow well from seed and at $2 a seed pack are inexpensive. Zinnias come in many shapes and colors—dwarf, tall (up to 4 feet), quill-leaved cactus and spider. You can buy multicolored seed blends specifically for cutting. Butterflies love tall, red or hot-pink zinnias in a large patch; 'Big Red' is a good choice. Zinnias do best in full sun with well-drained soil.

Vinca

Vinca (*Catharanthus*) are sun-loving plants that produce masses of flowers offset with glossy, green leaves. Growing 6 to 16 inches tall, vinca is a good choice for edging paths and borders and is also a great container or window box planting. Plant seedlings in spring after all danger of frost has passed. Vinca is drought tolerant but enjoys moderate moisture most. Vinca is self-cleaning, meaning you don't need to deadhead—it's that carefree! Enjoy deep-red flowers with sparkling white eyes with 'Jaio Dark Red.'

Globe Amaranth

The red variety of globe amaranth (*Gomphrena globosa*) is the rich color of tomato soup. This easy-to-grow annual loves hot conditions and blooms nonstop until frost. The pompon flowers are preferred for cutting and drying, and feel dry to the touch. Globe amaranth also attracts butterflies and is best planted in masses. It's not a fussy plant and tolerates a variety of soils and moisture levels.

ANNUAL PROFILE
BEGONIA

Annual begonias are so easy to grow and offer so many colorful options, including red, white, pink, coral and orange. Begonias are versatile and do well in a variety of conditions but prefer light shade, rich, well-drained soil and lots of water. There's no need to deadhead because they are self-cleaning.

'BELLFIRE' Crimson-pink flowers glow like embers against green foliage.

'BELLAGIO PINK' A double-flowering begonia imparts a lush look.

'DRAGON WING' This fast-growing annual fills in quickly and blooms until frost.

Melampodium
Marigold

Celosia

Lantana

COLORFUL ANNUALS: YELLOW

Warm up your garden or window boxes with sunny annuals that bloom in yellows, oranges and all the hues in between.

Melampodium

The irrepressible daisylike flowers of melampodium (*Melampodium*) brighten up any border or bed. This plant grows about 1 foot tall and makes a lovely little hedge because of its compact growth habit. Melampodium loves hot weather, but it must be well-watered or it wilts. It's also an excellent plant for containers because of its endless parade of cheery yellow flowers.

Marigold

The sunny upright plants of marigolds (*Tagetes patula*) are a delight in any garden. French marigolds bear frilly flowers and grow 8 to 12 inches tall. Although many varieties of marigolds are yellow or orange, several feature orange-red splashes such as 'Disco Queen' and 'Durango Red.' All marigolds do best in full sun with moist, well-drained soil. Try 'Yellow Gate' for large-flowered marigolds—3-inch flowers are borne on 1-foot-tall stems.

Celosia

Showy celosia (*Celosia plumosa*) comes in several flower forms. The plumed type, 'Fresh Look Yellow' (*opposite*), produces upright, flamelike spires of bloom. The crested type forms a fascinating twisted flower that somewhat resembles coral. Plant 'Armor Yellow' for a crested yellow flower. Both types are great in bouquets and also dry easily. Plant seedlings in spring after all danger of frost has passed. Celosia likes rich, well-drained soil with moderate water. This sun-loving annual blooms in yellow, orange and red.

Lantana

Lantana (*Lantana camara*) is a shrub in mild climates, but for everyone else this vigorous, flower-covered plant is an annual. 'Lucky Pot of Gold' lantana (*opposite*) can take the heat, thriving with little moisture and in full baking sun. The flowers are like little bouquets—some umbels have more than one color. (Try 'Irene' for yellow, pink and red flowers.) Lantana flowers all summer and into autumn, when it will be covered with monarch and swallowtail butterflies. Hummingbirds like it too. It's great in the landscape, and one plant fills up a big container. It grows 4 feet tall and spreads 4 feet wide.

ANNUAL PROFILE
RUDBECKIA

Originally a prairie plant, rudbeckia is also known by the common name black-eyed Susan. From midsummer on, these tough native plants bloom like crazy in sun or light shade. Add black-eyed Susans to wildflower meadows or native plant gardens for a truly natural look. Average soil is sufficient for black-eyed Susans, but the soil should be able to hold moisture fairly well. There are annual and perennial versions of rudbeckia. For example, 'Goldsturm' rudbeckia is a perennial and was named 1999 Perennial Plant of the Year.

'INDIAN SUMMER' Flower heads measure 6 inches across.

'RUSTIC DWARFS' Short in stature, this variety blooms with rust-stained petals.

'MAYA' This is a shaggy-flowered, sunny-yellow charmer.

Viola

Cosmos

Pinks

Fuchsia

COLORFUL ANNUALS: PURPLE & PINK

The pretty pastel colors of purple and pink add cottage charm to the garden. From ground-hugging violas to lacy-leafed waving cosmos, there are a wide range of annual options in this hue.

Viola

For cool-weather color, try any member of the viola (*Viola* x *wittrockiana*). From tiny Johnny-jump-ups to the stunning 3-inch blooms of Majestic Giant pansies, violas offer soft color and old-fashioned flowers in early spring. Plant violas in garden beds, containers, window boxes—anywhere you need a spot of cheery color. They can't take the heat, so replace them with heat-loving annuals when they start to wane.

Cosmos

A cottage-garden favorite, cosmos provides clear pink, purple and white flowers borne on long stems. Plants grow 2 to 5 feet tall, and the lacy foliage makes an elegant backdrop for shorter plants. Cosmos is a fast grower (making it a cinch to grow from seed) and a self-seeder, so you may only have to plant it once. It thrives with average moisture but will tolerate drought. *Cosmos sulfureus* bears yellow, orange and red single-petaled flowers.

Pinks

The annual pinks (*Dianthus chinensis*) are members of the dianthus family, also referred to as carnations. Pinks flower from spring to fall in sunny to partially shady spots. They bloom in pink, red and white and grow 6 to 18 inches tall.

Fuchsia

Exotic and beautiful, *Fuchsia* flowers are among the most intricate. The hanging lanternlike blooms come in magenta, pink, purple and white. Fuchsias are tender perennials grown as annuals outside tropical regions. They prefer well-drained soil and ample moisture, do best in areas with cool summers and don't like heat, humidity or drought. Fuchsias in a hanging basket should be placed in a sunny or partially sunny spot where wind doesn't bat the basket about.

ANNUAL PROFILE

COLEUS

Just when you think you know coleus, another variety comes out that changes your whole view. This species has it all: vivid color, wild markings, distinctive leaf shapes. There are coleuses engineered to thrive in the sun; 'Schizophrenia,' 'Sedona' or 'Solar Flare' offer beautiful, brightly colored foliage. When frost is around the corner, take 6-inch cuttings, put them in a glass of water on a windowsill and let them root. Pot them up and enjoy them as houseplants in a sunny window until spring, when you can replant them outdoors.

'DARK CHOCOLATE' This variety thrives in both sun and shade.

'ROYAL GLISSADE' Bright-green new growth fades to rich purple.

'THE LINE' Lime-green foliage is etched with a dark-purple band down the center.

Bacopa

Dusty Miller

Sweet Alyssum

Petunia

COLORFUL ANNUALS: WHITE

Light up your yard with a wide variety of white annuals. Perfect for gardens after dark, white-flowering and foliage plants offer great and glowing choices for beds and borders.

Bacopa

Lacy leaves and delicate white blooms make bacopa (*Sutera cordata*) a popular plant for hanging baskets and window boxes. Tiny five-petal flowers smother the long, cascading stems. Plant in full sun and keep well watered if in a container. Bacopa also makes an amazing groundcover because it spreads up to 3 feet across.

Dusty Miller

The silvery-white leaves of dusty miller (*Senecio cineraria*) are a great mixer with any color of flower or foliage. The finely cut foliage is this plant's best asset; the flowers are insignificant. Dusty miller is very easy to grow—it withstands heat, is drought tolerant, and deer won't go near it. Grows up to 2 feet tall.

Sweet Alyssum

Dainty, fragrant flowers that look like fine lace make sweet alyssum (*Lobularia maritima*) a popular annual for border edging and containers. Sweet alyssum spills over the edges of window boxes and planters, creating a soft, frothy look everywhere you plant it. But it's well behaved and won't cover paths by midsummer. Sweet alyssum does best in the cool temperatures of spring and fall and stops blooming in the heat of summer.

Petunia

If you're looking for a fail-proof flower, plant petunias (*Petunia*). They grow happily from mid-spring through late fall. 'Wave' petunias have made this plant even more popular. Reaching up to 4 feet long, they are a vigorous groundcover but really show their appeal in window boxes and pots. All petunias grow bushier if you pinch or cut them back by about one third to two thirds in midsummer. Another plus is that petunias are available in lots of colors. Many varieties are also scented.

ANNUAL PROFILE
VERBENA

Cute clusters of small blooms make annual verbena (*Verbena* x *hybrida*) a winner. It loves to spread out so it's an ideal choice for planting on the tops of retaining walls. In pots, baskets and window boxes it can cascade away. Plants prefer well-drained soil but are fairly drought-tolerant. Plant in full sun.

'QUARTZ SILVER' Pure-white blooms light up window boxes and containers.

'IMAGINATION' This robust grower takes on the hottest and driest conditions.

'FUEGO RED EVOLUTION' Jewel-toned flowers add sizzle to any garden.

HOW TO BUY: annuals

- Avoid leggy plants—tall seedlings have been in their pots too long.
- Pick stocky plants in bud, not in full flower.
- Slip seedlings out of their containers—if there are large masses of roots with little visible soil, it's a sign they've been in pots too long.

Heliotrope

TOP 5 MOST FRAGRANT ANNUALS

Nicotiana
Heliotrope
Stocks
Tuberose
Four O'clocks

Pinks

SUN LOVERS

COOL-SEASON ANNUALS

Calendula
Corn Poppy
Larkspur
Pansy
Pinks

WARM-SEASON ANNUALS

Million Bells
Celosia
Dusty Miller
Gazania
Mexican Sunflower

Coleus

SHADE LOVERS

COOL-SEASON ANNUALS

Annual Lobelia
Fuchsia
Mignonette
Monkey Flower
Nemesia

WARM-SEASON ANNUALS

Begonia
Browallia
Coleus
Impatiens
Wishbone Flower

HOW TO CREATE AN ANNUAL FLOWER BED

1. PLAN YOUR BED Make an outline for your garden bed using flour, or spray-paint the grass with biodegradable paint. Remove the sod and add amendments such as compost or composted manure.

2. SET OUT PLANTS Before you start planting, set out all your plants where you want them.

3. TEASE THE ROOTS Remove the plant from the container and break up the root ball to encourage growth. It's okay to rip the roots. Dig a hole the same size as the root ball, and plant.

4. APPLY MULCH A 2-inch-deep layer of mulch deters weeds and helps conserve moisture. Water new plants well.

"Hurray for spring! Bring on the tulips, daffodils—and the beginning of gardening season." —Emma

Flowering Bulbs: Easy Care in All Seasons

Bulbs are a special class of plants that produce big blooms from small packages. Flowering bulbs come in all sizes, from ground-hugging anemones to 6-foot-tall lilies. And they bloom in a wide range of colors and exotic flower forms. But all bulbs have one thing in common—they have an underground storage system for nutrients that powers their growth and fuels their blooms. Inside each bulb is nearly everything the plant needs to sprout and flower. In fact you can slice open a hyacinth bulb and see the tiny flower, like an embryo, inside.

Bulbs come in hardy and tender varieties. Spring-flowering bulbs are hardy, meaning they can withstand cold temperatures. In fact they require the cold. They are planted in the fall and wait out the cold winter months snugly underground. The indomitable spirit of spring-blooming bulbs is the reason so many gardeners are head-over-heels in love with these plants. If you plan your spring bulb plantings, you can enjoy flowers for about 100 days. From early-blooming crocus to the purple balls of *Allium* 'Giganteum,' spring bulbs offer spectacular style and an ever-changing palette of colors and flower forms.

Most summer-flowering bulbs are tender and cannot survive harsh winter conditions. The one exception to this rule is lilies: Many summer-flowering lilies are hardy and can be planted in either fall or spring. To enjoy summer-flowering bulbs, plant them in the ground or in containers in the spring and enjoy their blooms and foliage all summer long. If you want to replant them next year, dig them up in the fall before frost and store them indoors over the winter.

LEFT Daffodil, summer snowflake, pink lamium and purple viola combine to create a lush early-spring border.

RIGHT Spring-blooming bulbs must be planted in the fall so they can spend the winter underground.

Crocus

Grape Hyacinth

Summer Snowflake

Tulip

BULBS FOR SPRING

Early-blooming bulbs are simply amazing—some have evolved to bloom so early that they often push up through snow to show their stuff. Hardy and resilient, spring bulbs bloom from February through May.

Crocus

You'll fall in love with these perky flowers. Often poking up through the last drifts of snow, crocuses (*Crocus vernus*) are one of the first spring bulbs to bloom. Their chalice-shaped blossoms look best when planted in masses under trees and shrubs. You can even tuck individual bulbs into your lawn for a spring surprise. Crocuses thrive in well-drained soil in full to partial sun. Zones 3 to 8.

Grape Hyacinth

So called because their blooms resemble little grape clusters, grape hyacinth (*Muscari*) spreads electric-blue color throughout the spring landscape. Although blue and purple are the most common shades, grape hyacinth also blooms in white and yellow. These easy-care bulbs are often planted en masse to create a "river" effect throughout borders. The bulbs are about the size of a dime and produce 3- to 8-inch-tall plants that spread easily in any well-drained garden soil. Zones 3 to 8.

Summer Snowflake

An underused but very beautiful plant, the 2-foot-tall summer snowflake (*Leucojum aestivum*) sprouts in lovely green clumps of spearlike foliage topped with delicate, white-belled flowers; each petal is dotted a green spot. These European natives also bear a light scent. Despite their common name, they actually bloom in mid- to late spring. They spread easily, tolerate wet soils (unlike many other bulbs) and like full sun to partial shade. Zones 4 to 9.

Tulip

The quintessential flower of spring, tulips (*Tulipa*) range in size from small to tall (4 inches to 30 inches). Tulips also offer a variety of flower forms from classic chalice-shaped to those with fringed edges and wild, birdlike petals (parrot tulips). The first to bloom in the spring are low-growing species (or wild) tulips. Tall Triumphs add graceful color. Short Darwins are great for edging walkways or planting in rock gardens. Plant tulips in well-drained soil in either full sun or partial shade. Zones 3 to 9.

BULB PROFILE

NARCISSUS

If you grow just one type of bulb in your garden, narcissus should be your pick. It is easy to grow, nearly pest-proof (deer and rabbits snub it) and blooms reliably every spring. Commonly called daffodils, they bloom in a range of colors that include yellow, white, orange and pink. Grows in zones 3 to 9.

'BARRETT BROWNING' This small frilled orange trumpet surrounded by white petals grows 16 inches tall.

'THALIA' Sweetly scented ivory-trumpeted blooms open in pairs on tall stems. Grows 10 inches tall.

'WHITE LION' Ruffled, double-ivory and golden-yellow flowers bloom in mid-spring. Grows 20 inches tall.

Canna
Caladium
Calla
Dahlia

BULBS FOR summer

Just as the early spring bulbs are fading, summer bulbs rush in with great colors, flower forms and fragrance. Lilies are the queen of the summer border and come in a wide range of hues and types of flowers.

Canna

Enjoy a taste of the tropics with the bold blooms and foliage of cannas. Clustered, flaglike flowers top 2- to 6-foot-tall plants. Showy 'Australia' presents deep purple foliage and scarlet flowers. 'Pretoria' flaunts yellow-striped leaves with orange blooms. Dwarf cannas are also available for container gardening and small spaces. If you garden in a climate colder than Zone 9 (7 for the hardier types of cannas), you'll need to dig up canna plants and store them bareroot for the next season. Zones 7 to 11.

Caladium

Brighten up shady spots in your garden with the splashy leaves of caladium. Heart-shaped leaves display colorful veined patterns in colors that range from cream to neon pink, red, silver and green. Plant caladium tubers shallowly in pots, and water sparingly until sprouts appear. They grow vigorously in warm weather. Because they are tropical plants, they must be dug up and stored in a frost-free area. Zones 10 to 11.

Calla

Beautiful as cut flowers, the funnel-shaped blooms of callas (*Zantedeschia*) represent cool elegance in the garden. White varieties nearly glow in the dark and are perfect for night gardens. Callas also bloom in a rainbow of hues, including lavender, purple, orange, yellow and peach. Plants go dormant in colder winter areas of their hardiness range and do not emerge until temperatures warm up in late spring. Outside their hardiness range, store the rhizomes in a frost-free place for winter. Zones 7 to 10.

Dahlia

Blooming in a wide range of flower styles, sizes and colors, dahlias are a versatile mid- to late-summer flower. From petite mignonettes to gigantic dinner-plate varieties, these tender bulbs offer color possibilities for any garden or container. Pinch off the first crop of side flower buds to encourage branching and larger flowers. Gardeners in climates colder than Zone 8 should cut back the withered foliage after the first frost and dig up tubers to store over winter. Zones 8 to 10.

BULB PROFILE
LILY

Bright flowers, long bloom period, lovely scent—lilies have it all. From early summer to early fall lilies strut their stuff. To have the longest bloom time, grow some of each type, including Asiatics and the fragrant Orientals and *longiflora* hybrids. Lilies spread well and do best in light, fertile soil with good drainage. Plant in either fall or spring and they'll bloom the next summer. Lilies are hardy, so they can remain in the ground within their specified zones. Grow in zones 4 to 8.

LILIUM X LANCIFOLIUM Also called tiger lily, this is a good choice for northern gardens. It blooms from August to early September and grows 6 feet tall.

LILIUM SPECIOSUM Pink to red flowers dangle from 5-foot-tall stems.

'ENCHANTMENT' ASIATIC LILY It bears brilliant orange trumpets speckled in red and grows 3 feet tall.

Colchicum

Fall Crocus

Winter Daffodil

Spider Lily

BULBS FOR autumn

As the garden winds down for the summer, there are still surprises in store when you've planted fall-blooming bulbs. Some, such as colchicums, are planted in the fall and bloom that same season.

Colchicum

Colchicum (*Colchicum autumnale*) are sometimes called autumn crocus, although this is a misnomer. (There *are* crocus species that bloom in autumn.) Producing purple, pink or white flowers that resemble the chalice shape of spring-blooming crocuses, these plants emerge from September to October. Zones 4 to 9.

Fall Crocus

The delightful little flowers of fall crocus (*Crocus speciosus*) appear in October, growing up out of the ground beneath fading perennials. Plant in open areas so you don't miss them. They grow 4 to 6 inches tall. Zones 3 to 8.

Winter Daffodil

Bright-yellow winter daffodils light up the fall garden. *Sternbergia lutea* grows 6 inches tall. Plant bulbs in midsummer to late summer in a spot that receives full sun to partial shade. Position bulbs 3 inches apart and plant 5 inches deep. Zones 7 to 9.

Spider Lily

Also called surprise lily, the blooms of *Lycoris radiata* are indeed shocking when they pop up and open, seemingly overnight. This flower has another common name, naked ladies, because the flowers appear without leaves. The exotic-pink trumpet blooms sit atop 2-foot-tall stems. Zones 4 to 11.

BULB PROFILE
ORIENTAL LILY

Blooming in late summer and early autumn, Oriental lilies are large, lavish and long-lasting. Multiflowered blossoms are borne on tall stems and are very fragrant. Even the long stamens are richly colored. Zones 3 to 8.

'STARGAZER' One of the most popular varieties, it grows 3 feet tall.

'CASA BLANCA' Pure white, this very fragrant flower is beautiful in a vase. Remove pollen-covered (and staining) stamens.

'MUSCADET' Speckled pink blooms are beautiful as a back-of-the-border flower.

'Chico' Amaryllis

'Ludwig Dazzler' Amaryllis

'Apple Blossom' Amaryllis

'Red Lion' Amaryllis

BULBS FOR WINTER

You can enjoy the beauty of tender bulbs by forcing them indoors. Amaryllis are classic holiday décor—they even come in the holiday colors of white and red as well as pink, yellow, cream and peach. And paperwhite narcissus scents your entire house.

Amaryllis are easy to grow. Select a large, firm bulb (or order from a reputable mail-order source), which is more likely to produce multiple bloom stalks. Before you plant, soak the bulb roots in a shallow pan of lukewarm water for three to four hours. Select a pot that's twice as tall as the bulb to allow ample room for root growth. Fill the pot with potting soil, insert the bulb and add more soil. Water well but do not soak the bulb. Place the potted amaryllis in a sunny window. The bulb will send up a flower stock that will be topped with four trumpet-shaped blooms.

After the blooms fade, cut off the stem. A second stem may appear that also will be topped with blooms. If you want your bulb to rebloom the following year, set it outdoors once the threat of frost has passed and let it enjoy the summer sun. Keep it watered, but don't allow the soil to become too soggy. Before frost in the autumn, bring the amaryllis bulb indoors and store it in a cool, dark place. About a month before the winter holidays, set the pot in a sunny window to encourage reblooming.

'Chico' Amaryllis
Curving and tousled petals make this red and green amaryllis a real looker.

'Ludwig Dazzler' Amaryllis
Snow-white flowers bloom 6 to 8 weeks after forcing.

'Apple Blossom' Amaryllis
White petals are kissed with soft pink.

'Red Lion' Amaryllis
Dark-red blossoms make this amaryllis a holiday favorite.

BULB PROFILE
PAPERWHITE NARCISSUS

Paperwhite narcissus is a tender version of the daffodils you grow in your garden. Paperwhites can be forced to flower indoors any time of year. Pick a clear glass or plastic vessel in which to plant your bulbs. They don't even need soil—you can force the paperwhites in water alone. Just add enough to cover the lower portion of the bulbs without submersing them.

Paperwhites can grow in a variety of creative media that provide root support. Settle the bulbs in stones, marbles, beads or colored glass. Place each bulb so that half to three-quarters of it shows above the surface of the medium.

Set the bulbs in a warm, sunny spot and water regularly; they will flower in a month or so. For longer-lasting blooms, move the bulbs to a cool spot out of direct sunlight once the flowers appear.

HOW TO BUY: BULBS

Buy the largest bulbs for the species—"top size" is the biggest.

Look for healthy, plump, firm bulbs. Avoid spring-blooming bulbs that are withered or soft.

BULBS BY SIZE

LOW-GROWING (4 TO 8 INCHES)
Crocus
Snowdrops
Scilla
Species Tulips
Anemones

MEDIUM HEIGHT (1 TO 3 FEET)
Daffodil
Allium
Leucojum
Calla
Lycoris

TALL (4 TO 5 FEET AND TALLER)
Oriental Lilies
Cannas
Dinnerplate Dahlias
Fritillaria imperialis
Gladiolus

TOP 5 MOST FRAGRANT SPRING-BLOOMING BULBS

Hyacinth 'Sky Jacket'
Grape Hyacinth
Narcissus 'Thalia'
Narcissus 'Geranium'
Tulip 'Angelique'

'Sky Jacket' Hyacinth

HOW TO PLANT SPRING-BLOOMING BULBS

Bulbs start showing up in garden centers and nurseries around Labor Day, but that's too early to plant in all but the coldest climates. The best time to plant is about six weeks before the ground freezes. In most areas that's October and November.

1. SAVE YOUR BACK A soil auger attached to a battery-powered drill allows you to add bulbs to an existing flowerbed with minimal disturbance. Use this planting method for big bulbs such as tulips, daffodils and alliums.

2. PLANT IN GROUPS Tulips and narcissus planted in dense groups make a colorful impact in spring gardens. Space bulbs a bit closer together than the planting instructions suggest to get a denser show of color.

3. PLANT THE RIGHT DEPTH Each bulb type has a specific depth at which it must be planted. Using a bulb planter with a measure allows you to make sure you're planting each bulb correctly.

4. FEED AND WATER Add fertilizer when you plant bulbs to give them a jump start. Bonemeal, bulb food or compost work well. And make sure to water bulbs after you plant them.

1

2

3

4

"My house has no landscaping and my yard looks really bare and sad. Where do I start?" —Penny

Trees and Shrubs: Leafy and Lush

Flowers infuse your garden with color, but there are more than just colorful blooms in the horticultural paint box. Trees and shrubs can provide clouds of blossoms, fine foliage, fragrance, fruit and most important, structure.

Like giant bouquets for the landscape, flowering shrubs open up with a bang in spring. Lilacs unfurl their spired blooms to scent your yard with delicious perfume. Spirea's frothy flowers transform a simple foundation planting into a soft lace frill around your home. In the warmer areas of the country, azaleas and rhododendrons offer masses of vivid crepe-paper blossoms—a colorful announcement that spring has arrived. And fountains of yellow spray from forsythia and kerria shrubs brighten even the darkest corners of a yard.

The flowers of spring-blooming trees are just the first act of color in the landscape because for many species, such as viburnum, serviceberry and crabapple trees, the blooms are followed by brightly colored berries or fruits. Serviceberry's purple berries are a feast for hungry birds, such as robins and cardinals. And viburnum's glowing red clusters ripen late in the summer to feed nonmigratory birds that overwinter in your yard.

Large deciduous trees give structure, focal points and shade to your yard. Unless you have a lot of cash to spend on a really large tree, choose a smaller, less expensive version—no taller than 6 feet. Smaller trees grow and adapt quickly. Since most yards have limited space to accommodate many trees, it pays to invest in the right species. The best landscape trees look good in all seasons.

Shrubs and trees are fairly maintenance free. Woody plants, both deciduous and evergreen, take root easily when planted in the spring or fall and grow without much care or attention. You should stake newly planted trees, especially if they are in an open, windy area. And winter protection is important for trees with thin bark—such trees are susceptible to sunscald and rabbit damage. A spiral plastic tree wrap protects against both. Conifers, which are prone to moisture loss, can be wrapped for protection in winter.

Plant shrubs and trees that fit your yard size, sense of style and maintenance requirements. Trees produce (and drop into your yard) all sorts of things—fruits, nuts, berries and leaves. Locate trees with fruit away from patios and parking areas to avoid staining problems. If you're not interested in raking leaves in the fall, steer clear of deciduous trees (those that lose their leaves) and plant conifers instead.

Evergreen shrubs, such as Alberta spruce, add structure to your garden and color to your yard in all seasons.

Lilac
Dogwood
Spirea
Viburnum

COLORFUL SHRUBS

Nothing chases away the last vestiges of winter faster than flowering shrubs. Not only are these plants beautiful, they also attract wildlife such as birds, butterflies and bees.

Lilac

Lilacs (*Syringa*) offer gorgeous, richly scented flowers (called panicles) that bloom in purple, pink, blue, white and yellow. Lilacs range in height from 3 to 20 feet. For small spots or containers, try dwarf varieties, such as 'Palibin' or 'George Eastman,' that grow 4 to 6 feet tall. If you have the space, tall-growing old-fashioned lilacs are a treat. Plant a hedge of them for a spring spectacular of bloom followed by a lush green screen all summer. You even can plant upright tree forms of lilac. *Syringa reticulata* 'Ivory Silk' grows 12 feet tall and 6 feet wide and produces creamy-white flowers in early to midsummer. Lilacs prefer a sunny site and well-drained alkaline soil. Zones 2 to 9.

Dogwood

Most dogwoods (*Cornus*) produce small flowers that are followed by gorgeous globular fruits in white, red or purple. (Birds love them!) *Cornus racemosa,* (*opposite*) is an upright native shrub with white spring flowers that develop into clustered white fruit in summer. Other dogwoods offer showy, brightly colored stems that add winter interest. *Cornus alba* 'Elegantissima' features gray-green leaves edged in white on bright-red stems. Zones 3 to 8.

Spirea

Cascading branches filled with small white or pink flowers make spirea (*Spiraea*) a great mixer in flower borders. *Spiraea japonica* 'Anthony Waterer' blooms in spring, achieving a compact 3-foot-tall mound covered with deep-rosy-pink flowers—a beautiful companion for spring bulbs. For disguising unattractive foundations, nothing beats the old-fashioned favorite commonly called bridal wreath. *Spiraea prunifolia* 'Plena,' (*opposite*) bears tiny double white flowers on bare branches early in spring followed by glossy green leaves. Other types have colorful light-green or gold foliage. Spireas do best in a fertile, moist soil with good drainage. Zones 5 to 9.

Viburnum

Viburnum (*Viburnum*) offers a wide range of shapes, sizes, foliage and flower choices. *Viburnum trilobum* is a North American native that features flat, white lacecap-type blooms in spring and edible red fruits and maplelike green leaves in summer. It grows 15 feet tall and 12 feet wide. Chinese snowball viburnum (*Viburnum macrocephalum*) offers pompon clusters of snow-white flowers in late spring. This rounded deciduous shrub can also be trained as a small tree. Plant viburnums in fertile, moderately moist, well-drained soil. Zones 2 to 9.

SHRUB PROFILE
HYDRANGEA

Each flower of the hydrangea is a bouquet. This shade-loving shrub produces stunning clustered flowers in several forms: mophead (big balls) to lacecap (flat umbels) and panicle (swirling spires). Varieties differ in plant size, flower type and color and bloom time—from summer through fall. *Hydrangea macrophylla* are revered for their blue- or pink-balled blooms. The change in flower color results from lower pH and higher aluminum content in the soil. To get bluer flowers, adjust your soil's pH to the 5.2–5.5 range with aluminum sulfate. Hydrangeas thrive in a moist, fertile, well-drained soil in partial to full shade. Zones 4 to 9.

BIGLEAF HYDRANGEA
The pH of your soil changes the flower color.

PEEGEE HYDRANGEA
These plants grow into small trees with white flowers that turn russet.

OAKLEAF HYDRANGEA
The plant produces stunning flowers with handsome red fall foliage.

Birch

Burning Bush

Maple

Staghorn Sumac

COLOR FOR autumn

Fire up your yard with color when you need it the most—at the very end of the gardening season. Enjoy the best of fall foliage in your own yard.

Birch
One of the most elegant and graceful garden trees, birches (*Betula*) feature open, airy branches, textured trunks and brilliant-yellow fall color. The river birch is native to the U.S., and it's among the easiest to grow. Birches can be used as single trees in a landscape, but they're also beautiful when planted as an allée (in rows on either side of a path), in a grove or near water, where their impact is doubled in reflections. Sweet birch (*Betula lenta*), (*opposite*), is a dark-barked tree that grows 50 feet tall and 40 feet wide. Zones 2 to 7.

Burning Bush
Fiery-red fall foliage is the way this euonymus (*Euonymus alatus*) earned its name. This ornamental shrub features almond-shaped green foliage in the spring and summer and attractive reddish-purple berries. Burning bush can grow 20 feet tall and 10 feet wide. Euonymus does best in fertile, moist, well drained soil. Planting note: Some euonymus varieties are considered invasive pests in some regions; check local restrictions before planting them. Zones 4 to 8.

Maple
You get it all with a maple tree: cool shade, great shape and dramatic fall color. And happily, there's a maple (*Acer*) for just about every garden. Small varieties stay under 20 feet tall while big species reach 100 feet or more. Some maples have showy bark and branch texture (such as paperbark and coralbark maples). 'Autumn Blaze' maple (*Acer freemanii*), (*opposite*), is a popular tree with great color, dense branching, and disease and insect resistance. Zones 3 to 9.

Staghorn Sumac
This popular sumac (*Rhus typhina*) features branches that resemble deer antlers, hence its name. In autumn the 6-inch-long leaves turn a dark crimson with tinges of orange and yellow. Staghorn sumac reaches 25 feet in height. Zones 4 to 8.

TREE PROFILE JAPANESE MAPLE

Small with elegant branches and leaves, Japanese maples make excellent focal points or additions to garden borders. As understory trees, they can grow in shade or sun. There are a wide variety of different sizes, branching types and leaf shapes and colors, so you can find a Japanese maple that fits anywhere in your landscape. *Dissectum* or laceleaf maples generally have a weeping or mounding growth habit and finely cut leaves. *Linearilobum* or bamboo-leaf maples feature narrow leaves. Zones 5 to 8.

ACER PALMATUM 'BLOODGOOD' A fall foliage standout, this maple grows 20 feet tall.

ACER PALMATUM DISSECTUM Rarely growing taller than 6 feet, this maple and has lovely intricate leaves.

ACER JAPONICUM This tree provides good fall color and features deeply lobed leaves.

Boxwood

Arborvitae

Juniper

Yew

all-season color: evergreens

Evergreens are trees and shrubs that keep their green, needlelike leaves, making them great plantings for year-round gardens. You'll appreciate the structure and color they provide in a snowy winter landscape.

Boxwood

A standard hedging plant in formal gardens, this evergreen shrub (*Buxus*) can take on whatever shapes you want: a neat mound, a square hedge or big balls of foliage. Boxwood can be clipped into a 4-inch hedge or grow to 15 feet tall. Frequently used to create topiaries, this shrub bears small, green leaves that remain all winter, making it an excellent plant for four-season interest. Boxwood prefers full to partial sun. It does well in containers too. Zones 5 to 8.

Arborvitae

If you're looking for a lush screen in a northern climate, arborvitae (*Thuja*) may be your answer. This evergreen features luxuriant, fan-like foliage. Plant columnar forms, such as 'Pyramidalis,' in a hedge to create a green screen of privacy or a windbreak. Arborvitae also can be clipped into shapes and topiaries. Try bronzy 'Hetz Midget,' a dwarf variety that grows in a compact globe. Another small-space favorite is 'Little Gem' which grows 3 feet tall. Arborvitae like moist fertile soil and full sun. Zones 5 to 9.

Juniper

Fast-growing junipers (*Juniperus*) are ideal shrub solutions for many landscaping needs. Low-growing varieties make great groundcovers, and columnar types are good screens or hedges. Their foliage is feathery and graceful-looking but prickly, making it a good choice for barrier plantings. Creeping junipers, such as *Juniperus horizontalis* 'Blue Rug' feature trailing, silver-blue foliage that turns pale purple in winter. 'Blue Rug' is the perfect planting for rock gardens. Junipers thrive in full sun, and most are drought tolerant once established. Zones 3 to 9.

Yew

Evergreen yews (*Taxus* x *media*) have soft, fine-textured needles that stay dark green all year. For added color, female plants feature bright-red berries called arils. There are a wide number of different types of yews—ranging in size from 3 to 25 feet—that offer plush texture for dense hedges and living privacy screens. Yews can be clipped in any shape you want, as well as into topiaries. Plants do best in fertile, well-drained soil, growing well in sunny and shaded sites. Zones 4 to 7.

TREE PROFILE
DWARF CONIFERS

For small landscapes and containers, dwarf conifers give you all the color and texture of big trees in compact packages. Essentially, dwarfs conifers are slow-growing varieties of regular conifer species. For example, a white pine might grow 75 feet tall in 40 years while a dwarf white pine might never be taller than 5 feet.

A. Hinoki Cypress
(Chamaecyparis obtusa)
B. Dwarf mugo pine
(Pinus mugo 'Donna's Mini')
C. Cypress
(Chamaecyparis pisifera 'Cumulus')
D. Dwarf Alberta Spruce
(Picea glauca 'Pixie Dust')
E. Dwarf Alberta Spruce
(Picea glauca 'Jean's Dilly')

HOW TO BUY: TREES AND SHRUBS

- Inspect the leaves for wilting, discoloration, breakage and insect infestation.
- Look for well-spaced branching.
- For trees, avoid v-shaped crotches because they are more likely to break as they grow larger.
- Check roots and trunk. They should be firmly rooted in the container. They should have a solid, unbroken root ball if wrapped in burlap.

FLOWERING TREES AND SHRUBS BY BLOOM COLOR

BLUE/PURPLE
Hydrangea
Ceanothus
Lilac
Rhododendron
Buddleja

PINK
Weigela
Oleander
Spirea
Azalea
Redbud
Magnolia
Rose of Sharon

WHITE
Viburnum
Hydrangea
Spirea
Fothergilla
Crape Myrtle
Dogwood

YELLOW
Forsythia
Kerria
Potentilla
Witch Hazel
Azalea
Hibiscus

TOP 5 MOST FRAGRANT SHRUBS

Lilac
Magnolia
Honeysuckle
Winter Daphne
Mock Orange

Lilac

HOW TO PLANT A TREE OR SHRUB

The hardest part of planting a tree or shrub is digging the hole. After they're in, they require minimal care—just watering, occasional fertilizing and mulching.

1. DIG A HOLE Dig it no deeper than the height of the root ball and twice as wide. This leaves firm, undisturbed soil in the bottom of the hole and prevents plants from sinking as the soil settles.

2. POSITION THE PLANT Remove the shrub or tree from its nursery pot and drop it into place. Backfill with soil.

3. MAKE A MOAT After planting and refilling the hole, make a moat in the soil surrounding the tree or shrub to help hold water. Water deeply.

4. PROTECT THE PLANT Add a tree guard to protect it from sunscald.

5. GIVE SUPPORT Stake your tree if it is planted in an open and windy location. A swaying trunk breaks the feeder roots. Leave about an inch of give in the fastener. Larger trees can be staked using three guy wires arranged in an equilateral triangle.

1

2

3

4

5

"What's more beautiful than a rose? I want a whole garden filled with them." —Jacqueline

Abundant Roses: Romance on a Stem

From the beauty of a single flower to an arbor covered in blooms, roses add color and romance to your yard and garden. There is a rose form to suit every gardening need. All you require is a sunny spot to grow this classic flower. Here are a breakdown of popular types:

Shrub roses come in all shapes and sizes, from compact 3-foot-tall varieties to sprawling 15-foot-wide plants. They're hardy and vigorous growers that bloom repeatedly and are disease resistant. Shrub roses flower in lovely clusters and are low-maintenance choices for landscapes and gardens. For roses that provide vertical floral displays, ***climbing roses*** are the perfect choice. Long, pliable canes can be trained onto walls, pillars and arbors. Miniature climbers grow 3 to 6 feet tall. Large-flowering climbers grow 4 to 12 feet tall. And ***rambling roses*** can reach 20 to 30 feet in length.

As their name suggests, ***floribundas*** produce a lot of flowers. In fact the Latin translation of floribunda is "many-flowering." Low-growing and relatively hardy, floribundas are easy to raise and offer diversity of bloom types and colors. ***Hybrid teas*** display classic rose blooms. Perfect in almost every way, the hybrid tea bloom starts out as a tight, attractive bud that unfurls to a breathlessly perfect flower. Hybrid tea roses are tall and upright, with sparse foliage toward the base. Plants grow 4 to 6 feet tall.

Grandifloras blend the best traits of hybrid teas and floribundas. They produce blooms as elegantly shaped as hybrid teas, but in long-stemmed clusters that continually repeat, like a floribunda. The plants grow up to 6 feet tall and are hardy. ***Miniature roses*** grow 3 to 18 inches tall and offer the same colors and glossy leaves of other roses, just in a small package. These roses are extremely hardy.

Species roses are the original "wild roses" and are the ancestors and hybrids of modern roses (hybrid teas, floribundas, grandifloras). Species roses are single, having just five petaled blooms. They bloom in spring and bear rose hips in autumn, providing food for birds.

Climbing roses can smother an arbor or building in fragrant blooms. Plant at the base of a wall, fence or arbor, and a climbing rose will draw itself upward.

English Roses

Miniature Roses

Groundcover Roses

Climbing Roses

color your yard: roses

No matter what kind of garden you have—formal, cottage, contemporary—there's a rose that fits your garden style. They even grow well in containers.

English Roses

English roses offer petal-packed flowers and have some of the same characteristics as antique roses—with a distinct improvement. Their ability to repeat bloom makes English roses a good choice for cutting gardens. Their full, perfumed flowers make elegant but casual bouquets. David Austin roses offer romantic rose fans a full range of colors. Zones 4 to 9. See more David Austin roses on *page 92*.

Miniature Roses

You don't need a small-space garden to appreciate miniature roses. As edging plants in big gardens or growing in containers, these mighty minis offer colorful, perfectly shaped tiny blooms on clean, healthy plants. Most miniature roses grow less than 2 feet tall. Zones 4 to 11.

Groundcover Roses

Low-growing groundcover roses are useful for mass plantings and mix well with perennials or shrubs in borders. Plant them around the foundation of your home to add a floral frill. Popular groundcover roses include Flower Carpet roses; these bear loads of clustered blooms and have glossy, dark-green disease-resistant foliage. Plants grow up to 3 feet tall and 4 feet wide. Zones 5 to 10.

Climbing Roses

Climbing roses have long canes that can be trained to grow on pillars, fences, arbors and gazebos. They develop large, single flowers or clustered blooms on a stem. Depending on the variety, climbing roses may bloom once a season or continually. Zones 5 to 9.

ROSE PROFILE
'KNOCKOUT'

'Knockout' is known for its extreme disease resistance and great looks. If you leave the flowers on the plant, they form small orange rose hips that feed the birds. The plants grow about 3 feet tall in Zones 5 to 9.

'KNOCKOUT' This award-winning rose displays vibrant red petals and yellow stamens.

'RAINBOW KNOCKOUT' Pink petals surround a kiss of yellow at the center of the flower.

'BLUSHING KNOCKOUT' Frilly pink petals look stunning above this plant's dark-green foliage.

HOW TO BUY: ROSES

Bare-root roses: Buy dormant or leafed out. Roots are packed in peat moss; soak before planting.

Roses in containers: Look for plants with abundant foliage rising from several strong canes.

TOP 5 MOST FRAGRANT ROSES

'Memorial Day'
'Double Delight'
'Honey Perfume'
'Mr. Lincoln'
'Scentimental'

'Great Wall,' 'All the Rage,' 'Centennial' and 'Snowdrift' make a lovely bouquet.

ROSES FOR BOUQUETS

Singly or in big clusters, roses make the perfect bouquet. The best roses feature long stems and showy flowers.

RED
'Mr. Lincoln'
'Olympiad'
'Viva'

PINK
'Bewitched'
'Duet'

CORAL PINK
'Sonia'
'America'

YELLOW
'Gold Medal'
'New Day'

WHITE
'Honor'
'Iceberg'
'Pascali'

ORANGE-RED
'Marina'
'Ole'
'Prominent'

HOW TO PLANT A ROSE

Buy a bare-root rose or purchase a potted rose—either way you'll get great results if you follow these simple planting steps. If you are planting a potted rose, start at step 3.

1. UNPACK AND SOAK If you're planting a bare-root rose, remove the packing material and soak the roots in a tub of water for 2 to 4 hours. A cool bath helps the plant begin the process of waking up from dormancy.

2. TRIM THE ROOTS Trim the ends of the bare-root rose with a sharp pair of pruners to remove any broken or dead-looking ends. Also trim off any roots that are much longer than the others.

3. AMEND THE SOIL Dig a hole 2 feet wide and deep for a bare-root rose. For a potted rose, dig a hole 4 inches wider and deeper than the pot. Mix the soil that was removed from the hole with an equal amount of compost. Or mix in rose fertilizer as indicated on the package. Place about two-thirds of the amended soil in the planting hole, mounding it into a cone.

4. PLANT Set the rose on top of the mounded soil, allowing the roots to drape over the cone. Lay a shovel handle across the planting hole to make sure the graft line of the rose (a scarred area of the stem just above the root system) is above the handle. In zone 5 and colder, the graft should be an inch or two below the soil line. Fill in around the roots with the remaining soil. Water thoroughly and mulch.

"I'm looking for a way to soften the look of my yard (and hide my ugly foundation)." —Connie

Versatile Vines: Up, Up and Away

Able to leap tall heights, scramble horizontally or creep across the ground, vines are the superheroes of the garden. Perennial vines, such as trumpet vine, honeysuckle vine, wisteria, bougainvillea and clematis, offer flowering options that return year after year. If you want to swath your garden in green, try perennial foliage vines such as ivy.

Annual vines are a great way to try out a new vine every year. You plant them, they grow vigorously and flower like mad all summer, and when frost comes, they are done. Yellow-flowering black-eyed Susan vine is a cottage garden favorite. Sweet peas are sweetly scented and make great cut flowers. And morning glories twist and twine their way through fences and arbors, blooming all the way.

Tropical vines offer even more allure. Flowering jasmine vine is one of the most fragrant of all flowers; mandevilla offers extravagant trumpet-shaped blooms; and the exotic flowers of passionflower vine will stop garden guests in their tracks. There are even vines—grapes and kiwis among them—that add color to your arbors and fruit to your table.

Vines are excellent choices for small-space gardens because they grow vertically. Trained onto a trellis against a wall—or even growing in a container with a structure upon which they can climb—vines fill narrow spaces with blooms.

Plant two vines together and they'll intertwine joyously. Annual morning glory vine mingles with perennial 'Sweet Autumn' clematis.

Trumpet Vine

Honeysuckle Vine

Morning Glory

Black-Eyed Susan Vine

color your yard: vines

Scale new heights in your garden with vines. Train them onto fences, arbors and pergolas—or grow them in containers.

Trumpet Vine

This fast-growing, high-climbing perennial vine (*Campsis radicans*) can scale structures up to 40 feet tall. Hummingbirds and butterflies love the trumpet-shaped blooms that flower all summer long. The orange, red or yellow flowers form showy clusters that stand out against finely cut, dark-green leaves. Trumpet vine will grow in sun or shade but flowers best in sunny spots. This woody vine gets very heavy, so plant it on a sturdy structure. Zones 6 to 10.

Honeysuckle Vine

This easy-care perennial climber (*Lonicera*) presents attractive bloom clusters in a range of hues—pink, yellow, red. Hummingbirds adorc the tubular flowers. Honeysuckle vine is a good mingler, growing next to and intertwining with shrubs, perennials and annuals. It blooms all summer and climbs 25 feet. Zones 4 to 9.

Morning Glory

Create a blooming privacy screen by planting morning glory (*Ipomoea*) to grow on a trellis. Or perform a quick cover-up by twining morning glory onto a chain-link fence. This fast-growing annual vine produces a profusion of trumpet-shaped flowers that open in the morning and usually close by afternoon. Morning glories can self-seed, so don't be surprised if they show up in your garden the following year. Plants climb 12 feet.

Black-Eyed Susan Vine

Add bright color to your summer garden with vigorous-growing black-eyed Susan vine (*Thunbergia alata*). Most varieties bloom in yellow and orange. 'Little Susie' bears unusual white flowers with a chocolate-purple center. This well-behaved vine twines up a trellis or pole but doesn't try to wander off. It climbs 8 feet and is a perennial in zones 10 to 11, but elsewhere it is treated as an annual.

VINE PROFILE
CLEMATIS

You can't plant enough of this generous and delicate perennial vine. Few other climbers offer such a broad range of bloom colors—white, pink, blue, purple, yellow, burgundy and even pinwheel stripes. This hardy vine also produces a wide variety of flower types—doubles, singles, frilly-centered. And you can choose from plants of diverse flower sizes and bloom times. Grow dwarf clematis in containers or along decks if you have a small-space garden. Most clematis grow best in full sun and moist, well-drained soil. Zones 4 to 9.

'NELLY MOSER' Pink stripes! This cheerful variety blooms in both early and late summer and climbs 10 feet.

CLEMATIS X JACKMANII Choose this for the masses of dark-purple flowers all summer. It climbs 10 feet.

SWEET AUTUMN This fall-blooming clematis produces clouds of blooms. Tiny, white, single flowers offer sweet fragrance.

Sweet Pea

THE 6 MOST FRAGRANT VINES

Jasmine
Honeysuckle
Passionflower
Wisteria
Sweet Autumn Clematis
Sweet Pea

OTHER VINES FOR YOUR YARD AND GARDEN

Morning Glory

ANNUAL VINES

Hyacinth Bean
Cardinal Climber
Cup-and-Saucer Vine
Cypress Vine
Sweet Pea

Clematis

PERENNIAL VINES

Virginia Creeper
Wisteria
Boston Ivy
English Ivy
Dutchman's Pipe

HOW TO MAKE A TRELLIS

A trellis can do more than support a vine. Use it to decorate a wall or create a privacy screen. Make your own using 6- or 8-foot strips of 1 x 2 cedar and 1¼-inch screws.

1. DRAW A GRID Draw parallel lines 6 inches apart (and then perpendicular lines) on a concrete surface with chalk.

2. LAY OUT TRELLIS Create the trellis pattern using the chalk grid as a guide.

3. SECURE TRELLIS WITH SCREWS Wherever boards intersect, drive two screws. Do this from the backside so the heads won't be visible.

4. PAINT (OR NOT) AND HANG UP You can paint your trellis or leave it natural. Unpainted cedar will fade to a silvery gray.

"I want a lush but low-maintenance garden for the entryway and stairs leading to my front door." —Lisa

Groundcovers: Low-Growing Wonders

Groundcovers are a talented group of plants. Not only do they cover the ground with beautiful foliage and flowers, but their dense- and low-growth habit discourages weeds and prevents soil erosion. Groundcovers sport all different looks, colors and textures. Leafy groundcovers, such as ivy, pachysandra and vinca, can fill in open areas with lush greenery. Small-leaved spreading groundcovers easily carpet an area, making it feel spacious—much in the way that a lawn does—but without mowing maintenance. Flowering groundcovers, including moss phlox, sea thrift and prostrate veronica, provide colorful carpets of bloom. Groundcovers range in height from an inch tall to a foot or taller.

You can choose groundcovers that grow in compact little mounds. Non-spreading groundcovers, such as liriope grass and sea thrift, can be used as low hedges to flank walkways. Spreading groundcovers are like insatiable explorers, traveling in search of new ground. Eager spreaders, such as vinca or ajuga, can be a frugal gardener's best friend because just a few plants cover a large area with foliage and flowers.

With varieties that excel in sun or shade—and many that will tolerate a little of both—you can take your pick from a wide variety of groundcovers to accent your yard and garden. Shade lovers, such as wild ginger, will flourish where your lawn grass won't. Let a groundcover smother a slope so you don't have to mow it. Depending on your climate you can plant evergreen or deciduous groundcovers that look good all year.

Many herbs can be used as groundcovers. Thyme, oregano and mint will spread out—mint especially, so be careful. Try woody herbs such as creeping rosemary, a fragrant choice with culinary uses. Because of their low profile, groundcovers are frequently used as edging plants or front-of-the-border options, where they are a smooth transition between the lawn and garden.

A mix of leafy and flowering groundcovers adds color and texture to a stone-stepped entryway. Plants include sea thrift, New Zealand flax, oregano, sedum and thyme.

Creeping Veronica

Ajuga

Sea Thrift

Woolly Thyme

Color Your Yard: Groundcovers

Low-growing and spreading, groundcovers can fill in the blank spaces in your garden and landscape. Some groundcovers grow into thick mats of foliage that effectively choke out weeds and never have to be mowed. Flowering groundcovers become attractive carpets of color in shaded and sunny spots. And for rock gardens, small mounding or creeping groundcovers add color and texture.

Creeping Veronica

Creeping veronica (*Veronica umbrosa*) is a mat-forming flowering groundcover that does well even in poor soil. It grows 2 to 4 inches tall and is topped with vibrant blue flowers with perky white centers. Plant this prostrate veronica in spots in your yard and garden that receive full sun to partial shade. It's an ideal choice for crevices in rock gardens. Zones 4 to 8.

Ajuga

Ajuga reptans is an attractive leafy groundcover that comes in several colors—dark green with burgundy accents to lighter variegated cream-and-gold 'Golden Glow,' (*opposite*). Ajuga prefers shaded garden locations. The foliage is matlike and topped with spikes of blue flowers in late spring. Also called bugleweed, ajuga is hardy and carefree. It's drought tolerant, and deer pass it by. Zones 3 to 9.

Sea Thrift

Also called sea pink (*Armeria maritima*), this sun-loving rock garden favorite grows in grassy mounds topped with masses of round, pink flowers. Blooms appear in late spring, but if you keep sea thrift deadheaded, you'll enjoy flowers throughout the summer. The plants reach 6 to 12 inches tall. Plant in well-drained sandy soil. Zones 4 to 9.

Woolly Thyme

Low-growing woolly thyme (*Thymus pseudolanuginosus*) forms a cushy carpet of foliage in sunny spots. This gorgeous herb groundcover produces small, felted gray-green leaves that drape over rock walls and edging stones. It's an ideal choice for tucking into stone wall crevices, where it can cascade gracefully down a vertical surface. And woolly thyme can take foot traffic, so plant it between paving stones or near walkways. Zones 4 to 9.

6 Tips for a Gorgeous Lawn

A lush, green lawn is the perfect accent for flower-filled garden beds. Here are tips for keeping the lawn in great shape:

1. PLANT THE RIGHT GRASS In the north plant cool-season grasses such as Kentucky bluegrass, perennial ryegrass and tall fescue. In the south sow St. Augustine grass, Bermuda grass, centipede grass and zoysia grass.

2. BE SHARP A sharp blade cuts the grass; a dull blade shreds it. Sharpen your mower blade 2 or 3 times a year.

3. DON'T MOW TOO CLOSE Cut only a third of the grass blade when you mow. As the temperatures rise in the summer, raise the mower height.

4. WATER SMART The best way to water your lawn is uniformly, deeply—and infrequently. Water the lawn late at night or early in the morning so less water is lost to evaporation. Aim for 1 inch per week.

5. LEAVE CLIPPINGS Use a mulching mower to mince grass blades and leave them where they lie. Clippings provide nitrogen and organic matter for the soil. Contrary to popular belief, clippings do not contribute to thatch buildup.

6. BE ON WEED WATCH The best way to avoid weeds is to keep your lawn healthy. A robust lawn repels weeds.

Creeping Jenny + Variegated Sedum

THE 5 MOST "TREADABLE" GROUNDCOVERS

Irish Moss
Moneywort
Woolly Thyme
Dwarf Ajuga
Sedum spurium

OTHER GROUNDCOVERS FOR YOUR YARD AND GARDEN

Periwinkle

SHADE-LOVING GROUNDCOVERS
Periwinkle
Ajuga
Bloody Cranesbill
Moneywort
Lamium
Wild Ginger
Pachysandra
Ivy

Creeping Phlox

SUN-LOVING GROUNDCOVERS
Creeping Phlox
Lady's Mantle
Japanese Forest Grass
Hen-and-Chickens
Soapwort
Thyme
Sea Thrift
Sedum
Snow in Summer

HOW TO PLANT GROUNDCOVERS

Groundcovers are perfect planting solutions beneath trees, around stepping stones and in garden beds. Plant them anywhere you need a continuous swath of color or foliage.

1. GET EDGY Add a groundcover edging to create a footlight effect. 'Gold Teardrop' sedum turns on the lights.

2. ADD COLOR Low-growing groundcovers, such as alyssum, dianthus and moss phlox, infuse bursts of brilliance into rock gardens or tucked into a stone wall.

3. PLANT A RING Shade-loving groundcovers, such as bishop's weed, create a soft edge around large trees while eliminating lawn-trimming chores.

4. SHEAR BACK Some groundcovers, such as lamium, benefit from a shearing after they stop blooming to make them flower again later in the season.

Chapter Six
TOOLS AND ESSENTIALS

Gardening isn't rocket science. All you need are a few tips and tools to grow a gorgeous garden.

RR-S

Gear up for Gardening

You don't need a potting shed filled with dozens of tools to be a successful gardener. What you do need is good soil and a few essential items to create and grow your dream garden.

Start with good soil. Your soil is home for your plants. Add generous helpings of organic matter, such as compost you can buy or make yourself, and you'll ensure that your plants have the nutrients they need to thrive. Even if your soil isn't ideal, you can add amendments to your beds and borders that will result in great-looking and healthy plants.

Dig, plant, prune, water, mulch. There are certain standard actions you do in a garden, and there are efficient (and back-saving) tools to help you complete nearly every job. The type of gardening you do and your personal preferences dictate the tools you need. You may want to have a low-key garden and use simple but efficient hand tools. Or you may want to power up and take advantage of gardening machines such as tillers and edgers.

Buy quality tools. If you buy good tools, they will last for a long time. A stainless-steel spade is virtually indestructible. A good pair of pruners will last for many years. Although you can find inexpensive tools (and you may be tempted to purchase them when you first start gardening), you'll find that quality tools, while pricey, will outperform cheaper tools and last through many gardening seasons.

Gear up for your garden. The types of tools you need depend on the type of gardening you do. If you have a small raised-bed perennial border, you'll need digging tools (a border spade) to plant large perennials, a trowel to plant small annuals, a hand pruner to cut flowers and deadhead plants, and a long-handled lopper to handle cutting jobs for small tree and shrub limbs. If you plant a large garden, you may want to invest in power equipment such as a tiller that turns the soil every spring (saving your back). If you have a large hedge you like clipped to a certain style, an electric hedge clipper is a good purchase.

Dress the part. Gardening involves physical work. Just as you gear up at the gym with the right shoes for running, goggles for swimming or a comfortable yoga mat for stretching, gardening has its own group of useful accessories. A good pair of gardening gloves is invaluable to keep your hands and nails from looking rough. Purchase gloves with reinforced fingertips and palms, which are the areas that wear through first. If you'll be working with thorny plants, such as roses, gear up with gloves that are thicker than gardening gloves and that feature protection all the way up to the elbow. Gardening clothes should be lightweight and comfortable. Some gardeners prefer all-cotton because it breathes. Depending on the mud level in your garden, you may want to choose footwear from garden boots to clogs. You should select footwear that lets you move easily and without constraint. Shoes or boots that can be sprayed clean with a hose and dry quickly are always a plus. A gardening hat is a must for protection from the sun as well as to keep your hair out of your eyes as you lean down.

Shield against the sun. While your tomatoes need six hours of sun per day, you don't. Schedule your gardening activities early in the morning or later in the day so that you avoid the sun's most intense rays (from 10 a.m. to 2 p.m.). Be sure to apply sunscreen before you go out to the garden. Most gardeners lose track of time (because gardening is so fun and absorbing!), and it's easy to stay out in the sun longer than you planned. It doesn't have to be clear for you to get too much sun—you can get burned even on an overcast day. When you work in your garden, cover up. Wear gloves and a hat to protect your ears and neck. (A hat will also keep your hair from getting too much sun, a must for color-treated hair.) Use sunscreen on exposed skin. Keep a bottle of sunscreen in your gear bag or potting shed for easy applications. A good lip gloss is important too, especially on windy days. Protect your eyes with sunglasses. Buy a good-quality version coated with a UVA blocking filter.

Planting annuals and perennials in healthy soil gives them the nutrients they need to bloom and flourish all season.

Grow Your Garden: SOIL

The key to gorgeous flowers and pumped-up plants is the soil they grow in. They need rich, loamy soil that nourishes and supports them.

Start with good soil, and your garden will reward you with healthy, happy plants. The type and quality of your soil affect how well your plants will grow—and how much extra time you will spend working in your garden.

All soil is not equal. The ideal soil is loam, a humus-rich balance of silt, sand and clay. Healthy soil is easy to dig in, well-draining so it isn't boggy and has enough organic material to hold moisture to hydrate plant roots. How do you know what kind of soil you have? Start with a soil test. You can buy a kit and do it yourself or you can send a soil sample to your state extension service. A soil test measures the levels of nutrients (nitrogen, phosphorus and potassium) in your garden.

The test also will tell you your soil's pH level, which is the measure of its acidity or alkalinity. Your soil's pH affects how plants thrive. Soil pH ranges from 1.0 (acid) to 14.0 (highly alkaline), with 7 being neutral. In certain regions soil is typically more acid (in rainy regions) or more alkaline (in desert areas) and needs to be amended accordingly for plants to thrive.

To raise too-low (acidic) pH, add lime, dolomite limestone or wood ashes. To lower too-high (alkaline) pH, add horticultural sulfur, composted oak leaves or pine needles.

EASY DOES IT
SOIL PREP

Here are some guidelines for ensuring nutrient-rich, easy-to-plant-in soil:

FIX YOUR SOIL FIRST For long-term success it's better to feed the soil than the plant.

FEED IT EVERY SEASON Feed your soil in spring, summer and fall and every time you plant, using organic matter such as compost, rotted manure and chopped leaves.

TAKE THE CRUMBLE TEST Work soil when a fistful of it crumbles easily in your hand. Don't dig in your garden when soil is too wet or too dry because that damages the soil.

TREAD LIGHTLY Don't walk on your beds. Stepping on soil compacts it, preventing air, water and nutrients from reaching plants.

DON'T OVERDIG OR TILL Excessive digging or rototilling destroys the soil's structure, leaving it powdery or rock hard.

BUILDING BETTER SOIL

GYPSUM Powdered mineral that loosens heavy and clay soil; improves drainage.

PERLITE White volcanic residue that aerates soil and lasts indefinitely. Good for all soil types; a little helps.

GREENSAND Powdered rock that contains potassium and other nutrients. Slows soil compaction and helps retain moisture.

SPHAGNUM PEAT MOSS Absorbs moisture; especially helpful in sandy soil. Loosens heavy or clay soils.

COMPOST/ MANURE Aged or rotted manure (from cows, sheep, horses, chickens and others) boosts soil nitrogen. It loosens heavy soil and improves water retention in light soils. Fresh manure burns plants; compost it for a year before using.

PEAT ELIMINATOR Made from ground coconut (which is called coir), it helps aerate clay soil.

Add a slow-release granular fertilizer around plants and work into the soil lightly with a hand fork.

Fertilizer

Fertilizer is food for your soil and adds fresh supplies of the three things that plants need to grow: nitrogen, phosphorus and potassium. Fertilizers are sold with varying ratios of these nutrients. You'll see the numbers on fertilizer packages (such as 5-10-5) that indicate the percentage of the following:

N = Nitrogen fuels leaf and stem growth.
P = Phosphorus stimulates root growth and seed formation.
K = Potassium promotes flowering, fruiting and disease resistance.

EASY DOES IT FERTILIZING

There are several ways to fertilize your garden:

FOLIAR FEEDING Dissolve a liquid or powdered water-soluble fertilizer in water. Spray or pour directly on leaves using a pump sprayer or watering can.

GRANULAR, SLOW-RELEASE FERTILIZER Sprinkle granular fertilizer on the soil in the spring, and it will feed garden plants all summer.

ORGANIC FERTILIZERS Organic fertilizers are formulated from a wide number of natural materials such as animal manures, fish meal, rock phosphate, seaweed and wood ashes. Nutrients in granular fertilizers may be derived from natural sources or synthesized in a laboratory. Synthetic nutrients are coated to slow down their release rate. Organic fertilizers release more nutrients into the soil in hot weather, when plants most need the boost.

A mix of decomposed leaves, grass clippings, plant-based kitchen scraps and other organic materials makes a rich and highly nutritious compost for your garden that helps to lighten heavy soils and enriches poor soil.

Grow Your Garden: COMPOST

When you cook up a batch of compost in your backyard, you are the ultimate multitasker: You recycle "green" yard waste AND you make free fertilizer to nourish your flowers. Green lawn debris, such as garden clippings, deadheaded flowers, dry leaves, kitchen vegetable scraps and small twigs, slowly and naturally decompose to create compost.

There are two methods of composting: cold and hot. To cold-compost, collect yard waste, such as grass clippings and leaves and organic materials, including fruit and vegetable peels, coffee grounds and eggshells, and corral them in a pile or bin. Over the course of a year or so, the material will decompose. Hot composting is much faster and allows you to make and use compost in the same gardening season. You need four ingredients: fresh "green" plant material, dry "brown" plant material, air and water.

To create your own organic hot-compost heap, collect material to make a pile at least 3 feet deep. Create alternating 4- to 8-inch layers of green and brown materials. Green materials consist of vegetable scraps, grass clippings and plant trimmings. Brown materials include dried leaves and shredded newspaper.

To help the composting process, sprinkle water over the pile regularly so it stays moist. Don't add too much water or the microorganisms that cause the decomposition will become waterlogged and won't heat the pile properly.

Turn the materials once a week with a garden fork. The best time is when the center of the pile feels warm or a compost thermometer reads between 130 and 150 degrees F. Stirring the pile helps it cook faster and prevents material from becoming matted down and developing a bad odor.

When the compost no longer gives off heat and becomes dry, brown and crumbly, it's fully cooked and ready to feed to the garden.

SAVE MONEY
MAKE COMPOST

GOOD GREENS FOR YOUR COMPOST
- Fruit scraps
- Vegetable scraps
- Eggshells
- Coffee grounds
- Grass and plant clippings

GOOD BROWNS FOR YOUR COMPOST
- Dry leaves
- Finely chopped wood and bark chips
- Shredded newspaper
- Straw
- Sawdust from untreated wood

AVOID ADDING TO YOUR COMPOSTER
- Anything containing meat, oil, fat, grease
- Diseased plant materials
- Sawdust or chips from pressure-treated wood
- Dog or cat feces
- Weeds that go to seed
- Dairy products

Bark Nuggets

Shredded Wood

Grass

Cocoa Hulls

Pine Straw

Rubber

River Rock

Slate

Lava Rock

Grow Your Garden: Mulch

Spreading mulch on top of your beds and borders helps eliminate weeding chores and retains soil moisture. Mulch also can help reduce erosion and protect plants in winter from temperature extremes. There are two kinds of mulch: organic and inorganic. Organic mulch includes bark, shredded wood, grass and other plant material. These materials look natural but decompose over time. Inorganic materials, such as rocks or rubber, are permanent and require little maintenance.

Bark Nuggets
Bigger than shredded wood bits, bark nuggets are an organic mulch that takes longer to decompose than shredded wood.

Shredded Wood
Made from trees that include cedar, cypress and pine, wood is the most popular mulch. It comes in different colors—from light brown to red and dark brown.

Grass
Clippings from your lawn mowing have two good things going for them—they are free and readily available all summer. Don't use clippings as mulch around plants if you use a broadleaf weed killer on your lawn. Shredded leaves also make a good free mulch.

Cocoa Hulls
Small and attractive, cocoa hulls are excellent mulch for small plantings such as herbs. Because they're organic, they decompose, so you'll have to reapply. Cocoa hulls may blow around because they are lightweight. If you have dogs, you may want to avoid using this mulch because they tend to eat it, and it can cause illness.

Pine Straw
Pine straw (pine needles) acidifies soil—so it's the perfect mulch for camellias and other acid-loving plants. Pine straw offers a beautiful natural look, like the forest floor.

Rubber
Old tires, shredded and recycled as mulch, look like dark shredded bark. Rubber doesn't break down, like organic mulch, so it lasts 10 years or more.

River Rock
Small and rounded, river rock comes in different sizes and stays put in flowerbeds. If used on top of landscape fabric, it is permanent mulch—an excellent choice for low-maintenance landscapes.

Slate
Dark-gray slate offers a monochromatic mulch that looks great in Asian gardens. Put it over landscape cloth, and you'll never weed again.

Lava rock
Porous and lightweight, lava rock comes in different sizes and colors. You can use lava rock to mulch the surface of container plantings to help retain soil moisture.

Garden Spade

Garden Fork

Garden Rake

Hoe

Shovel

TOOLS: LONG-HANDLED DIGGERS

Planting and cultivating are the two tasks that require good digging tools. Shovels, spades, forks and hoes all work the ground in different ways. Handle length is important in long-handled tools. You should try the tools out at the store before you buy them to make sure they're comfortable and the right size.

Garden Spade
This spade features a shorter handle and a flat, squared-off blade. Also known as a border spade, this tool is great for detail digging, such as edging a garden bed, working soil amendments into the garden and digging holes.

Garden Fork
A garden fork has four sharp tines that are excellent for digging into soil to turn it over or to break up soil chunks. A fork is the best tool to use to work amendments, such as compost, into the soil. It's also handy to divide perennials.

Garden Rake
Made of tough steel, this 12- to 14-tined rake is used to smooth out a new planting bed and break up small soil chunks. You can flip the rake over to level the soil for planting.

Hoe
This long-handled tool features a small, straight-edged blade that allows you to cultivate the soil and remove small weeds around plants in a garden bed. It can be used to chop up soil chunks. Used at an angle, it makes a neat furrow for planting seeds.

Shovel
A shovel differs from a spade in that it has a concave blade with a tapered tip. That makes it the ideal tool for digging a hole and for moving piles of soil or sand.

EASY DOES IT
TILLER

A SMALL TILLER—either electric or gas-powered—makes quick work of a new garden bed. Ideal for mixing amendments into the soil, a tiller turns chunky ground into easy-to-plant-in soil. If you have a small garden but love the fast work that a tiller performs, think about renting one for a day. If you have gardening neighbors, considering purchasing a "community tiller" that the neighborhood can use. You generally only use a tiller in the spring to prepare a bed, but some tillers feature attachments that also allow you to cultivate your garden during the growing season.

Garden Claw

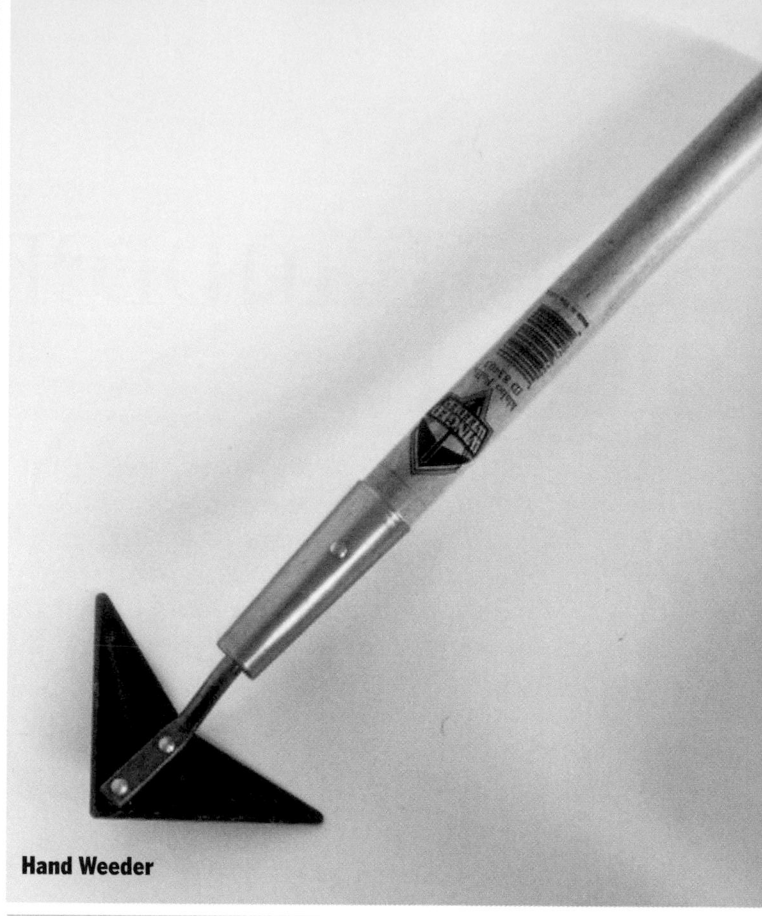

Hand Weeder

Hand Rake

Dibber + Bulb Planter

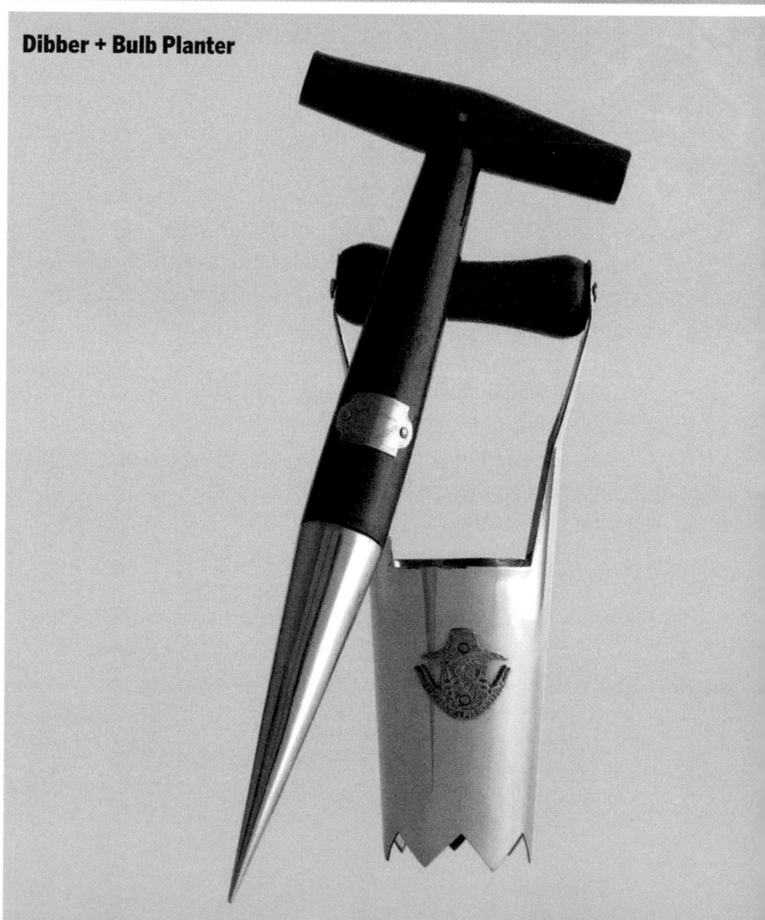

TOOLS: SHORT-HANDLED DIGGERS

If you have a small garden or lots of containers, there are several hand tools that you'll find indispensable. Today's tools are ergonomically designed to be less taxing on wrists, arms, shoulders and backs. Modern materials have made them extremely sturdy while also featherlight.

Garden Claw
It may look like something from a horror film, but a garden claw is a tool you'll find really useful. The bent tines scrape the ground, yanking up weeds and self-sown seedlings you want to remove.

Hand Weeder
For tougher weeding problems, try a hand weeder. Essentially a mini hoe, this tool features a straight-edge blade that severs weeds at or just below the soil's surface. If you turn the blade upward, you can use its sharp corner to dislodge stones or dig out larger weeds.

Hand Rake
Handy for cleaning up the garden in the spring, a hand rake dislodges leaves from around the base of perennials, trees and shrubs. The springy tines allow you to gather up leaves and debris without damaging the plants in the work area.

Bulb Planters
There are several ways to dig holes for bulbs. For little bulbs, such as scilla and crocus, use a dibber (sometimes also called a dibble). This sharp tool makes a small hole—perfect for one bulb. A bulb planter makes larger holes, more suitable for daffodils, tulips and alliums.

IF YOU ONLY OWN ONE
TRUSTY TROWEL

DIG IN This basic digging tool is used to plant seedlings, seeds, bulbs and small perennials. Trowels are available with different widths of blades. Try a couple before you commit to a favorite. If you want your trowel to last forever, get a stainless-steel variety.

HOW TO MAKE A FLOWER BED

1. OUTLINE THE GARDEN EDGE Use a garden hose to define the outline of your garden. You can also use a can of spray paint to mark the shape of the bed or border. Then use a spade to remove sod if in a grassy area.

2. ADD SOIL AMENDMENTS Improve the quality of your soil by adding organic material such as compost or peat moss. If you're not sure what kind of soil you have, get your soil tested with an easy-to-use soil testing kit.

3. WORK THE SOIL Add the compost or other amendments to the soil in the bed to make it easy to plant in and nutritious for your plants. Use a tiller or a garden fork to mix the soil and amendments together.

4. MAKE A GARDEN EDGE Dig out a flat area in front of the garden bed to make an edge that will be easy to mow. Use a brick turned sideways as the border's high edge (to keep the soil from spilling into the grass).

5. POSITION THE PLANTS Set the plants in position as your plan indicates. Refer to the mature size of the plant (how tall and wide it will get) on the planting tag and position it accordingly. Plant each of the plants.

6. WATER WELL Using a wand, water all the new plants deeply. New plants—even those that are drought resistant—need a good drink to help them become established.

7. MULCH THE BED Place a 2- to 3-inch layer of mulch around the plants in the bed. Use organic mulch, such as shredded bark or cocoa bean hulls, or inorganic mulch such as stones or gravel.

EASY DOES IT

Invest in a good pair of gardening gloves to keep your hands and nails clean. Gloves with reinforced fingertips will wear the longest.

Wavy Blade Hedge Shears
Pole Saw
Telescoping Lopper
Bypass Lopper

TOOLS: LONG-HANDLED CUTTERS

Trimming, deadheading, thinning out—these are just some of the gardening activities that require a good cutting tool. You don't need a separate tool for each action; however, you may find that a specialty tool is just what you need to get a particular job done.

Wavy-Blade Hedge Shears

The wavy-blade edges of these shears help hold the stems when cutting and shaping shrubs. These are the shears to use to make a good first cut. If you have a lot of hedge to trim, you may want to opt for an electric- or gas-powered hedge trimmer.

Bypass Lopper

The long handles of a bypass lopper give you the torque to slice cleanly through shrub and tree branches as well as woody perennials. The tool is best used on green branches that measure up to 1½ inches in diameter.

Telescoping Lopper

A telescoping lopper allows you to prune trees and shrubs that are taller than you are by extending your reach by almost 10 feet. Look for a cut-and-hold feature that lets you prune overhead branches without allowing them to fall as soon as they are cut.

Pole Saw

If you have a lot of trees that need cleanup, try a pole saw. Its telescoping pole allows you to reach and prune branches up to 12 feet away.

EASY DOES IT
PRUNING

FALL

CUT BACK BRANCHES that interfere with power lines.
PRUNE BACK ROSES to one-third the shrub size.
RESHAPE HEDGES that have become shaggy since their spring shearing.

LATE WINTER/EARLY SPRING

PRUNE SUMMER-BLOOMING SHRUBS by cutting back branches to healthy buds pointing in the direction you want the shrub to grow.
PRUNE TREES including fruit trees.

SPRING

WAIT FOR THE BLOSSOMS TO FADE on spring-flowering shrubs such as lilac, and then prune.
SHEAR HEDGES in spring or early summer.

ANYTIME

REMOVE DEAD, broken, weak or diseased stems.

Pruning Snips

Root Pruner

Folding Saw

Bow Saw

TOOLS: SHORT-HANDLED CUTTERS

For small cutting jobs, a hand tool is the best option. Pruning back perennials, removing small branches from trees and shrubs, root pruning and deadheading are all easy cuts with one of the right tools listed here.

Pruning Snips

Snipping and shaping is the cutting ability that pruning snips provide. This is the finessing tool to use after you've trimmed your hedge with wavy-blade shears. (*See page 281.*) These snips are a lot like scissors (and exactly the same tool that sheep shearers use to remove wool from sheep). Use pruning snips for detail trimming on fine-leafed plants such as boxwood, yew and arborvitae.

Root Pruner

When you need to sever a root while digging or transplanting, use a root pruner. This angled tool digs in with precision, helping you lift plants with deep or dense root systems. Plus it's small enough to tuck into your tool caddy, so you can carry it everywhere.

Folding Saw

A folding saw features large, sharp teeth that can cut through green wood with ease. It folds up, making it safe to store in your tool caddy. To trim dead wood, try a saw with smaller teeth.

Bow Saw

A bow saw features a narrow blade that cuts with both push and pull strokes, so it's very efficient. Use it to clip off small branches. This tool will last forever because you can replace a dulled blade with a new, sharp one.

IF YOU ONLY OWN ONE
HAND PRUNER

CUT UP Hand pruners are a garden essential and easily the most commonly used cutting tool. There are two styles of hand pruners: bypass and anvil. Bypass pruners (*top*) feature two precision-fit blades that slide past each other in a scissorslike action that cuts rather than crushes a stem. This is the best pruner for cutting stems for a bouquet, deadheading flowers and trimming small branches up to 1 inch in diameter. An anvil pruner (*bottom*) is less useful as a garden cutter. Instead of slicing to cut, it pinches a branch between its sharp straight blade and a flat non-cutting blade. This type of pruner is best for cutting deadwood up to ¾ inch in diameter.

Watering Can

Rain Barrel

Timer

Hose

Rain Gauge

Watering Wand

TOOLS: watering

Deep watering is best for your plants. When you water, do so thoroughly, letting the moisture soak into the ground where the roots need it. Don't merely wet the surface.

Watering Can
Classic and low-tech, a watering can is a simple vessel with a spout to help direct the water. The spout end is fitted with a "rose"—a perforated disk that converts the stream of water into a showerlike spray.

Rain Barrel
Gather water for free using a rain barrel. Set a barrel beneath a rain gutter or collect water from your roof. Rainwater provides a natural water source for your summer watering. Most rain barrel systems feature 50- to 70-gallon containers.

Timer
A faucet-mounted timer remembers to shut off your sprinkler so you don't have to. You can get a nozzle-mounted meter to help you keep track of how much water you're using while you're watering—it's a handy tool in places that have water-rationing rules.

Hose
A new, kink-resistant hose will make your life so easy (because unkinking a hose is a truly annoying task). Keeping your hose rolled up and off the ground will keep it in top shape.

Rain Gauge
Place a rain gauge in your garden to measure rainfall after a summer shower. You can measure water from your sprinkler if you use one—that way you can adjust the timer to give your plants and lawn exactly the right amount of water.

Watering Wand
A hose-attached watering wand provides a gentle spray perfect for giving seeds and small seedlings a drink. If you water your garden from overhead, do it early in the day so the foliage dries before nightfall. This will help avoid mildew problems for some plants.

EASY DOES IT
DRIP IRRIGATION

WATER EFFICIENTLY Drip irrigation is the most effective way to water garden beds. More efficient than overhead sprinklers, drip systems deliver water to plant root systems because the water goes directly into the ground, not onto the leaves. With this type of watering system, little water is lost due to dehydration. You can lay irrigation hoses throughout beds and borders—and there are even kits that can water groups of containers. A drip irrigation system is made from black plastic piping, with emitters along the length of the pipe that drip water directly into the soil. A soaker hose is a porous hose that "sweats" water along its entire length.

Edgers

Staking

Mulching Mower

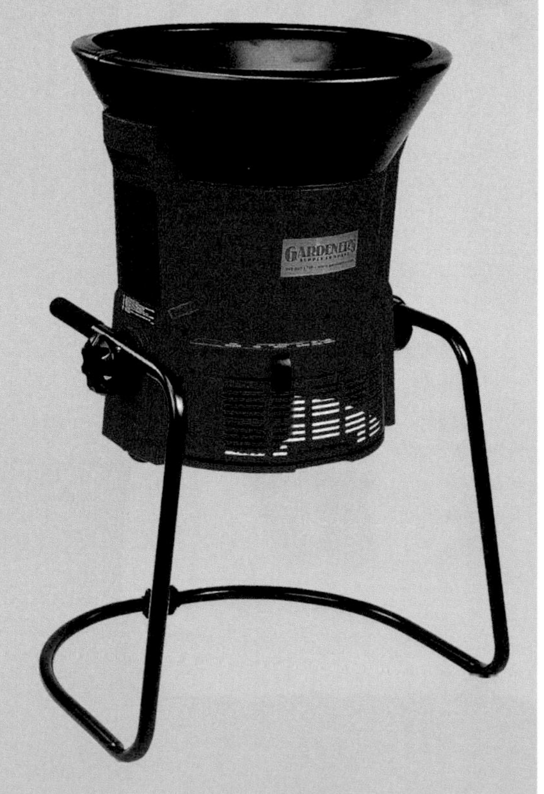
Chipper/Shredder

Leaf Blower

TOOLS: CLEAN UP

Sweeping, raking, clearing up—these activities don't take much time, but they make a world of difference in how your garden looks. Keeping your garden looking trim and clean is easy with the right tools. From staking plants to creating a defined edge around your garden beds to cleaning up fall leaves—you can keep your garden looking great with just a few hours of attention every week.

Edgers

A grass edge around a garden bed creates a beautiful foil for your flowers. But grass likes to spread, so creating a clean edge between lawn and garden is an important part of keeping your garden looking neat. Available in gas and electric models, edgers allow you to create a clean and weedless edge around gardens and walkways. Edgers create a defined trench by cutting weed and grass roots.

Staking

Keep tall plants from toppling over in wind and rain with a variety of staking options. Dahlias, delphiniums and peonies all look better and stay safer from breakage when they are staked. For tall-stemmed plants, use straight stakes and loosely tie the plant stem to the stake. For mounding but floppy plants, such as peonies, use staking rings. Set them in place in spring so the plant grows up through it and receives support from within.

Mulching Mower

If you have deciduous trees, you have leaves to clean up. The most low-tech method of leaf collection is the classic rake, and it's a perfect solution for small yards and gardens. But you also can use a mulching mower as a leaf shredder. Shredding leaves right on your lawn not only eliminates the need to bag them but also adds nutrients and organic matter to your grass.

Chipper/Shredder

Chop leaves and small twigs in a chipper/shredder, then spread them on your garden as mulch. Shredded leaves contain a small amount of nitrogen but offer your garden soil a rich source of calcium and magnesium. You can also shred branches and twigs into great material for rustic pathway coverings. Small shredders are available in electric or gasoline versions. Larger, gas-powered chipper/shredders have easy-to-use features, such as an electric start button, and wheels so you can roll them wherever they're needed.

Leaf Blower

Leaf blowers make quick work of gathering leaves into a pile for shredding or placing into recycling bags. Leaf blowers can clean up more than just leaves. Use them to blow clean patios, porches and brick and stone walkways. Some models are true multitaskers and will blow, vacuum or shred leaves.

Slugs

Rabbits

Japanese Beetle Traps

Deer

Deterring Aphids, Mites and Mealybugs

Garden Problems: Pests

The best way to keep your garden pest free—especially from munching insects—is to keep your plants healthy. Plants that aren't healthy or are stressed have fewer defenses against attack.

Slugs

These impressively voracious pests can defoliate a garden quickly. They eat large holes in leaves and leave behind a silvery slime trail, so it's fairly easy to know when you have them in your garden. Since slugs don't like being out and about in sun, they seek shelter under boards or rocks. Place a flat rock in your garden to lure them to shelter, then lift it every day and scrape them into a pan of soapy water. With a flashlight (and rubber gloves), you can hand-pick the slugs at night, which will greatly reduce their numbers.

Rabbits

Rabbits are really cute—until they dine on your garden. Rabbits will eat vegetable gardens and also the tender shoots of young plants, including shrubs. A fence is the most effective way to exclude rabbits from your yard. Welded wire mesh at the base of a fence will deter even small, young rabbits. For small flowerbeds you can make a lightweight frame and cover it with plastic mesh netting.

Japanese Beetles

Japanese beetles are small (about ½ inch long) but visible iridescent insects that dine on a variety of leafy plants. They are especially destructive to rose gardens, eating both the leaves and flowers. Japanese beetle traps baited with pheromone or floral lures attract and trap beetles. Place traps at the distant corners of your property, not in your garden, because you'll lure them in to eat your plants.

Deer

Gardeners spend a lot of time and effort to try to outwit these hungry grazers. Deer can denude a garden (usually of your favorite plants) nearly overnight, so keeping them out is important. Many products deter deer. Most are scent-based sprays or liquids that make an area or a plant undesirable to them. Others attempt to startle deer with sprays of water. But the best deer defense is a barrier—an 8-foot fence around the perimeter of your yard.

Aphids, Mites and Mealybugs

A simple water blast from the hose can control small, soft-bodied insects such as aphids, mites and mealybugs. A strong spray knocks them off the plant. You also can use insecticidal soap to kill these small insects.

INSECTS
GOOD GUYS

Good bugs in the garden help police the bad bugs. That's why killing all the insects is a bad idea. Beneficial insects, such as parasitic wasps, lacewings and ladybug larvae, actually eat the bad guys in your garden. Here are some of the bugs you want to welcome:

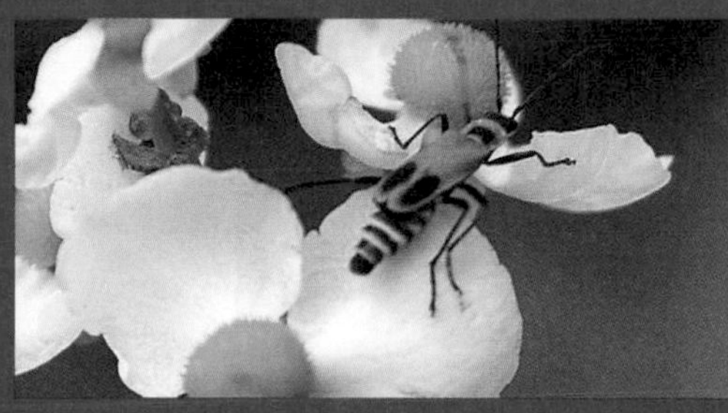

SOLDIER BEETLES feed on aphids, mites, caterpillars, grasshopper eggs, beetle larvae and other small garden pests.

SPIDERS help control pest insect populations by preying on those eggs in the soil.

PRAYING MANTISES don't make the distinction between pest insects and beneficial insects in the garden—they eat both.

Powdery Mildew on Phlox

Powdery Mildew on Columbine

Powdery Mildew on Sweet Pea

Black Spot on Rose

Bacterial Leaf Spot on Perennial Geranium

Garden Problems: Diseases

Spots, dots and white powder on the leaves—these are symptoms of a variety of ailments that can affect the plants in your garden. But just as you wouldn't put a cast on the leg of someone who has a broken arm, you need to investigate the problem and treat it with the proper solution.

Prevention—The Best Medicine

Strong and healthy plants are less likely to fall prey to insect infestations or disease. So your best defense against pests is preventive health care. Help your plants stay healthy by giving them what they need: the right light, suitable soil conditions, water and fertilizer. You also can select varieties that are particularly resistant to common problems. For example, *Phlox paniculata* 'David' is resistant to powdery mildew, a disease that frequently affects other phlox. Planting lots of different kinds of flowers and foliage plants creates diversity in your garden. So if you do have a problem with one type of plant, you most likely won't have it with your entire garden.

Powdery Mildew

This fungus makes your plants look as though someone sprinkled the leaves with flour. Powdery mildew dulls the vivid green of your garden and makes your flowers look less healthy. Full sun and good air circulation are the keys to avoiding powdery mildew. Thin plants and avoid getting the foliage wet, especially in the afternoon and evening, when moisture is less likely to evaporate. If your garden is susceptible to attacks, look for plant varieties that tout disease resistance. Otherwise use a garden fungicide specifically formulated for powdery mildew to control it.

Other Fungus and Disease

Black spot and crown rot also are fungal diseases. Black spot spreads quickly in warm, wet weather and is passed to other plants from diseased leaves that fall on the ground. Most fungicides won't cure black spot or crown rot, so prevention is the best option. Remove infected leaves before they drop off the plant to keep the disease from running rampant. Wet leaves encourage these and other fungal diseases, so avoid overhead watering and use a soaker hose instead. If you have had fungal disease in your garden, use a preemptive fungicide at the start of warm weather—before you see problems—to keep the disease at bay. Bacterial leaf spot occurs when there is plenty of moisture and warm temperatures. Avoid watering by overhead sprinklers to help prevent it.

PLANT PROBLEMS
DISEASE OR INSECTS

IDENTIFY SPOTS Spots on plant leaves usually mean your plant is infected with a disease, not overtaken by an insect infestation. There are some insects that can cause dark spots on leaves, and these spots usually appear in a pattern. Most dark spots on leaves are symptoms of fungal or bacterial disease that invades the leaf cells and spreads to form new spots. It is usually a disease rather than a pest problem if the edges of the leaf have become a different color from the middle.

DIAGNOSE DOTS Some tiny insects, such as aphids and spider mites, cause damage by sucking plant sap from leaves. They leave behind telltale pinprick-size yellow dots. These leaf suckers are usually found on leaf undersides.

LOOK FOR HOLES Insects generally chew the edges of the leaves or make holes between the leaf veins. Look closely at both the fronts and backs of leaves and within the petals of the flowers to discover the culprit. If the insects are really tiny, use a magnifying glass and you may see them.

TREAT THE PROBLEM There is a huge difference between fungicides (which kill fungi), insecticides (which kill insects) and herbicides (which kill unwanted plants). Be careful to diagnose the problem before pursuing treatment. Before you use an insecticide or fungicide, read the label to make sure it's safe to use on the plant you want to treat. Many insecticides are too toxic for edible plants. And some fungicides can damage plants, especially when used in hot weather.

Metal

Plastic, Resin and Foam

Glazed Ceramic

Wood

Concrete

Terra-Cotta

Garden Décor: Containers

With more choices than ever, gardeners can opt for a wide variety of container types, sizes and colors. You can mix and match containers or choose all the same kind. The only requirement is that they have a drainage hole in the bottom so the soil doesn't become waterlogged.

Metal

Containers made from cast iron will last forever—unless you drop and break them. Perfect for places where you don't want them to topple (around a pool, for example), cast-iron containers come in classic styles and are also pricey. You can enjoy cast iron in its natural rust finish or paint it to match your outdoor décor. You can buy lighter-weight (and less costly) copper sheet metal containers in a large number of sizes, styles and colors. Aluminum containers are the least expensive—and most lightweight—metal containers.

Plastic and Foam

A whole new world of plastic, foam, resin and fiberglass containers is here. Available in a wide range of colors and styles, these are also weather-resistant and lightweight. You can get old-world classic urns in plastic for a fraction of the price you'd pay for a cast-iron version. These containers are a good choice for large plants that need to be moved indoors at the end of summer (such as small citrus trees or jasmine vines).

Glazed Ceramic

If you like colorful containers, take a look at the choices you get from glazed ceramic. Essentially glazed terra-cotta pots, they offer outdoor rooms and garden settings a wide range of colors, from sapphire blue to emerald green and ruby red. Handle with care because they chip easily. If they don't have drainage holes in the bottom, you can drill them. Or use them as cachepots by slipping the grower's pots inside.

Wood

Most wood planters are constructed from naturally rot-resistant woods: cedar, hardwoods or decay-resistant tropical woods such as teak, ipe or shorea. You can plant directly into wooden containers. But make sure the seams are tight so soil doesn't wash out (along with the water you are adding to hydrate your plants). Planters with open slots, *opposite,* can be lined or used to hold smaller pots. Wood containers impart a natural look. To prevent wood rot, set containers on concrete or wood surfaces rather than on the lawn or ground.

Concrete

Cast concrete runs the style gamut from classical to modern. Also called cast stone, these containers are heavy. Once filled with soil, large containers may be impossible to move, so make sure you like where you place them. Concrete containers are somewhat limited in colors, but their designs can be amazingly ornate. Their cost is moderate to expensive—especially if you are buying large ones.

Terra-Cotta

Inexpensive, natural-looking and the classic plant container, terra-cotta can't be beat. Mexican terra-cotta is less expensive but also less weather-resistant than Italian terra-cotta. This is denser, fired at higher temperatures and longer lasting. With earthy good looks, terra-cotta containers come in all sizes. If you live in a cold climate, you'll need to bring containers inside in the winter so they will not freeze and crack.

Composites
Bricks
Stone
Plastic
Bottles
Decorative

Garden Décor: Edging

The area between your garden and your lawn requires definition. A good edge prevents grass runners from slipping into flowerbeds. Bricks, stone and other edgers with gaps require periodic removal of grass invaders. There are many good ways to edge a garden—the choice depends on the look you want. Here are some options:

Composites
Also known as decking material, this extremely durable option should be buried so the top edge is level with the lawn's surface.

Bricks
A good choice for formal gardens, brick edging offers a classic look. You can create any pattern. A brick edge allows a lawn mower wheel to ride on top, eliminating the need to trim grass by hand—which means less time spent on maintenance.

Stone
Like brick, stone (such as the limestone, *opposite*) can create an edge that a mower wheel can ride over.

Plastic
Widely used and misused, plastic edging can be unattractive if improperly installed. A plastic edge should be buried so only the rounded top is above the ground, and secured with stakes to resist frost heave. The design *opposite* doubles as an irrigation system.

Bottles
A low-cost and whimsical option, use upended wine, beer or soda bottles as an edging material. This is a great choice for casual, cottage or country gardens.

Decorative
Decorative fencing creates an attractive visual border but is not a barrier from grass.

SAVE MONEY
CUT-FACE EDGING

GET EDGY A no-cost edging you make yourself, a cut-face border edge is functional as well as neat looking. Trim the edge of your bed. Make clean cuts along the edge using a spade or a bed-edging tool (with a sharp, curved blade specifically for this task). Scoop out enough soil to accommodate a 3-inch exposed face, which will help keep your bed's mulch in place.

Off-the-rack sheds can be purchased pre-built or can be assembled on your property. The costs range from a couple hundred dollars to several thousand, depending on the size and features. Before building a potting shed, check with your local building inspector to make sure your plans are within the guidelines of your city's building codes.

Garden Décor: Potting Sheds

A small building in your garden offers a beautiful focal point and an ideal place to house all your gardening gear.

You can incorporate your potting shed into the landscape in a variety of ways. Place it at the end of your property and create a path leading to it so it feels like a destination. Or erect a potting shed at the end or side of your garden so it becomes a focal point. If your shed is near your house, you can match the color scheme (paint and roof shingles) and architectural details of your home. Or you can create a potting shed with its own theme.

A potting shed can have all sorts of decorative features, just like your home: window boxes, shutters, a weather vane, a cupola or even a patio. Decorative garden structures have long been popular. A folly—a small building that was really more decorative than functional—was a common garden ornament in English gardens of the 18th and 19th centuries.

Although the outside of your potting shed is decorative, the inside should be hardworking. Add shelves so you can conveniently store pots and containers. Fill shiny aluminum garbage cans with potting soil mixture and a scoop so you have everything you need at your fingertips when potting up containers. A pegboard and hooks will help you organize and store your tools for easy accessibility. And the requisite piece of furniture for a potting shed is a potting bench—a long table that is the perfect spot to plant seed flats and repot plants.

A shed with windows and a skylight can double as a mini greenhouse. If you're going to spend a lot of time working inside your potting shed, install screens on the windows and door for ventilation. Another way to make your shed more useful is to add electricity so you can run a heater or use grow lights to start seeds. If the shed has a tall ceiling, you might consider installing a ceiling fan to keep air moving.

A potting shed is more than just a building where you stash your gardening stuff; it also can be your own backyard getaway. For some gardeners a potting shed doubles as a spot to kick back and enjoy the garden. Turn the potting shed into a teahouse, with tables and chairs for entertaining. Or add a desk or large worktable to use the space as a writing or crafts room. Some sheds double as a home office or a spare bedroom.

POTTING BENCH
GARDEN WORK SPACE

WORK SPACE *AND* STORAGE A potting bench makes seed starting and potting up plants a snap. Most benches feature a waist-high surface so you can stand while working without bending over. Look for other useful options to fit your specific gardening needs. A built-in potting soil center is handy if you want to create your own potting soil mixes. Under-bench storage for cans that hold soil and amendments keeps all your supplies nearby. And back shelves, where you can store hand tools, plant markers and stacks of pots, also are useful. If you work in multiple areas in your garden, look for a potting bench with wheels.

POTTING SHED: elements

POT STORAGE
A shelf keeps breakable terra-cotta pots off the floor and out of the way until ready for use.

DOOR STORAGE
The inside doors of a potting shed are underused spaces that can be fitted with hooks and holders for tools that are used most often.

TOOL STORAGE
A pegboard equipped with hooks and hangers provides convenient space for all kinds of tools.

EASY-CLEAN FLOORING
Painted concrete flooring is easy to hose down or sweep up after potting chores.

PATIO PAVERS
Lay down a few flat stones to make a small patio area for containers and seating.

POTTING SHED ORGANIZERS

Your potting shed should be outfitted to accommodate all of your gardening activities, from seed starting to potting up containers and tool storage.

WHEEL RAMP
If you plan to store a wheelbarrow or a lawn mower in your potting shed, add a wheel ramp to make going in and out easier.

TOOL HANGUPS
Keep the gardening tools you use the most right at hand by installing hangers, pegs or hooks on the inside door of your potting shed.

SHELF STORAGE
Install pegboard paneling to add shelves to the inside of your potting shed. Store easily spilled bags of fertilizer and soil on the top shelf so they are out of reach of kids and pets.

Spring Start-Up

- **Start** seeds indoors under grow lights for warm-weather annuals, herbs and vegetables.
- **Remove** mulch from areas where spring-blooming bulbs are planted to help soil warm up to encourage blooming.
- **Divide** summer- or fall-blooming perennials.
- **Allow** flowering bulb foliage to die back—don't remove.
- **Set** stake supports over floppy plants such as peonies and near tall bloomers such as delphiniums. Set out tomato cages.
- **Start** summer-blooming bulbs such as cannas, caladiums and callas.
- **Till** garden beds and add amendments.
- **Sow** seeds or annual flowers and vegetables into soil once all danger of frost is past.
- **Replace** mulch where needed.
- **Install** a soaker hose or drip-irrigation system for more efficient watering of beds and borders.
- **Dig** new garden beds.
- **Harvest** spring cool-weather crops such as lettuce greens and broccoli.
- **Clean out** water garden.
- **Cover** tender crops to avoid frost damage.

Sow Seeds

Enjoy Blooming Crocus

Protect Crops

Deadhead Flowers

Harvest Tomatoes

Stake Tall Perennials

summer maintenance

- **Deadhead** faded flowers to stimulate continuous blooming.
- **Apply** slow-release granular fertilizer to beds and borders.
- **Plant** containers and window boxes with annuals and perennials.
- **Plant** warm-weather vegetables and herbs such as tomatoes and basil.
- **Inspect** plant leaves for pest problems.
- **Monitor** water garden for algae problems.
- **Plant** late-summer annual seeds.
- **Thin** self-seeded flowers, if necessary.
- **Check soil moisture** if rainfall is sparse. Water, if necessary.
- **Fill in** bare spots in perennials beds with blooming annuals.
- **Harvest** vegetables, herbs and flowers for drying.
- **Train** climbing vines and roses onto structures.
- **Stake** perennials that have grown too tall.

Fall Cleanup

- **Divide** spring- and summer-blooming plants.
- **Investigate** the fall colored shrubs and flowers in your neighborhood and plant your favorite varieties.
- **Plant** trees and shrubs.
- **Dig up** tender bulbs such as dahlias and gladiolus. Store in a frost-free location.
- **Plant** perennials.
- **Plant** spring-blooming bulbs such as narcissus and tulips.
- **Cut back** dead plants after a killing frost and compost them. Discard any plant material that appears diseased.
- **Spread** mulch over beds and borders.
- **Use** season extenders, such as cold frames and cloches, to protect cool-weather vegetables.
- **Winterize** the water garden.
- **Rake** leaves and layer them on your garden as mulch or compost them.

Plant Bulbs

Rake Leaves

Divide Perennials

Force Bulbs

Wrap Conifers

Add Outdoor Lighting

winter preparation

- **Wrap** conifers (evergreens) to protect them against drying winter winds.
- **Add** outdoor lighting to garden structures.
- **Check** mulch levels on beds and borders and reapply if needed.
- **Finish** spring-blooming bulb planting—you can plant after frost if the ground hasn't frozen yet.
- **Clean** and sharpen loppers, pruners and handsaws.
- **Clean** and store shovels and shades.
- **Organize** the potting shed.
- **Start** winter-blooming bulbs, such as paperwhites and amaryllis, for indoor flowers during the holidays.
- **Review** seed and plant catalogs for what to plant the following season.

THE USDA PLANT HARDINESS ZONE MAP

Each plant has an ability to withstand cold temperatures, called a hardiness rating. This range of temperatures is expressed as a zone—and a zone map shows where you can grow this plant.

Planting for Your Zone

There are 11 zones from Canada to Mexico, and each zone represents the lowest expected winter temperature in that area. Each zone is based on a 10-degree difference in minimum temperatures. Once you know your hardiness zone, you can choose plants for your garden that will flourish. Look for the hardiness zone on the plant tags of the perennials, trees and shrubs you buy.

Microclimates in Your Yard

Not all areas in your yard are the same. Depending on your geography, trees and structures, some spots may receive different sunlight and wind and consequently experience temperature differences. Take a look around your yard and you may notice that the same plant comes up sooner in one place than another. This is the microclimate concept in action. A microclimate is an area in your yard that is slightly different (cooler or hotter) than the other areas of your yard.

Create a Microclimate

Once you're aware of your yard's microclimates, you can use them to your advantage. For example, you may be able to grow plants in a sheltered, southern-facing garden bed that you can't grow elsewhere in your yard. You can create a microclimate by planting evergreens on the north side of a property to block prevailing winds. Or plant deciduous trees on the south side to provide shade in summer.

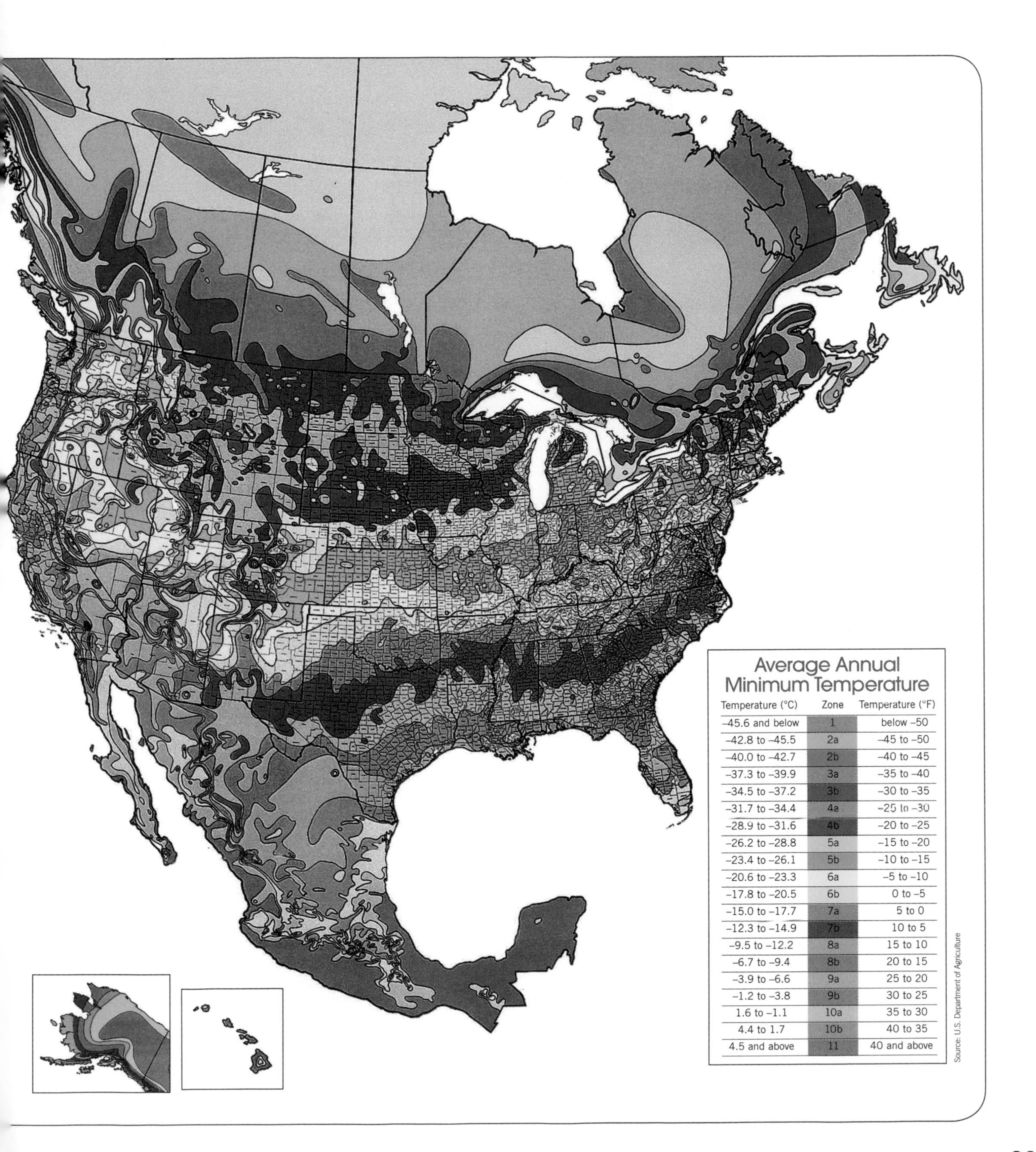

Temperature (°C)	Zone	Temperature (°F)
–45.6 and below	1	below –50
–42.8 to –45.5	2a	–45 to –50
–40.0 to –42.7	2b	–40 to –45
–37.3 to –39.9	3a	–35 to –40
–34.5 to –37.2	3b	–30 to –35
–31.7 to –34.4	4a	–25 to –30
–28.9 to –31.6	4b	–20 to –25
–26.2 to –28.8	5a	–15 to –20
–23.4 to –26.1	5b	–10 to –15
–20.6 to –23.3	6a	–5 to –10
–17.8 to –20.5	6b	0 to –5
–15.0 to –17.7	7a	5 to 0
–12.3 to –14.9	7b	10 to 5
–9.5 to –12.2	8a	15 to 10
–6.7 to –9.4	8b	20 to 15
–3.9 to –6.6	9a	25 to 20
–1.2 to –3.8	9b	30 to 25
1.6 to –1.1	10a	35 to 30
4.4 to 1.7	10b	40 to 35
4.5 and above	11	40 and above

BUYING GUIDE & resources

For information about sourcing seeds, plants and gardening products, contact these resources.

PLANT INFORMATION WEBSITES

Ball Seed
www.ballhort.com

Better Homes and Gardens
www.bhg.com

American Horticulture Society
www.ahs.org *703/768-5700*

American Rose Society
www.ars.org

Perennial Plant Association
www.perennialplant.org *614/771-8431*

International Flower Bulb Centre
www.bulb.com

MAIL-ORDER PLANTS/BULBS

Bluestone Perennials
www.bluestoneperennials.com *800/852-5243*

Brent and Becky's Bulbs
www.brentandbeckysbulbs.com *877/661-2852*

Busse Gardens
www.bussegardens.com *800/544-3192*

Forestfarm
www.forestfarm.com *541/846-7269*

Gilbert H. Wild & Son, L.L.C
www.gilberthwild.com *888/449-4537*

Greer Gardens
www.greergardens.com *800/548-0111*

High Country Gardens
www.highcountrygardens.com *800/925-9387*

Jackson & Perkins
www.jacksonandperkins.com *800/292-4769*

John Scheepers, Inc.
www.johnscheepers.com *860/567-0838*

Lilypons Water Gardens
www.lilypons.com *800/999-5459*

McClure & Zimmerman
www.mzbulb.com *800/546-4053*

Musser Forests
www.musserforests.com *800/643-8319*

Niche Gardens
www.nichegardens.com *919/967-0078*

Plant Delights Nursery
www.plantdelights.com *919/772-4794*

Tranquil Lake Nursery
www.tranquil-lake.com *508/252-4002*

Under A Foot Plant Company (Stepables)
www.stepables.com *503/581-8915*

Van Bourgondien
www.dutchbulbs.com *800/622-9997*

White Flower Farm
www.whiteflowerfarm.com *800/503-9624*

William Tricker, Inc. Water Garden
www.tricker.com *800/524-3492*

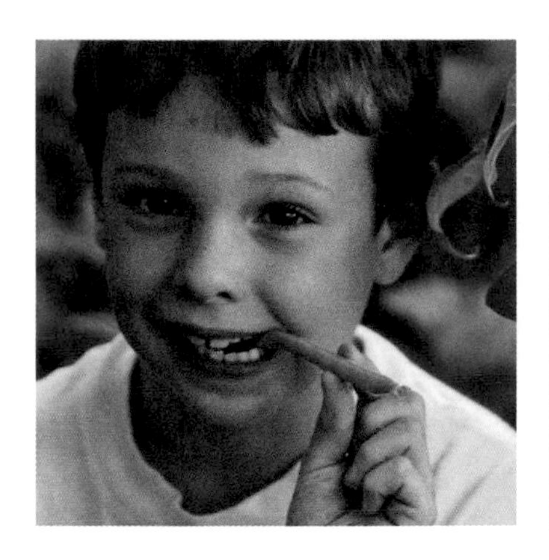

MAIL-ORDER SEEDS

W. Atlee Burpee & Company
www.burpee.com *800/333-5808*

Ferry-Morse Seed Company
www.ferry-morse.com *800/626-3392*

Gurney's Seed and Nursery
www.gurneys.com *513/354-1492*

Johnny's Selected Seeds
www.johnnyseeds.com *877/564-6697*

Nichols Garden Nursery
www.gardennursery.com *800/422-3985*

Park Seed Company
www.parkseed.com *800/213-0076*

Pinetree Garden Seeds
www.superseeds.com *207/926-3400*

Renee's Garden
www.reneesgarden.com *888/880-7228*

Richters
www.richters.com *905/640-6677*

Seeds of Change
www.seedsofchange.com *888/762-7333*

Seed Savers Exchange
www.seedsavers.org *563/382-5990*

Select Seeds
www.selectseeds.com *800/684-0395*

Stokes Seeds
www.stokeseeds.com *800/396-9238*

Thompson & Morgan
www.thompson-morgan.com *800/274-7333*

The Cook's Garden
www.cooksgarden.com *800/457-9703*

The Gourmet Gardener
www.gourmetgardener.com *386/362-9089*

ROSES

Antique Rose Emporium
www.antiqueroseemporium.com
800/441-0002

Anthony Tesselaar Plants
www.tesselaar.com *310/349-0714*

Conard-Pyle Co.
www.conard-pyle.com *800/458-6559*

David Austin Roses, Ltd.
www.davidaustinroses.com *800/328-8893*

Heirloom Roses
www.heirloomroses.com *503/538-1576*

High Country Roses
www.highcountryroses.com *800/552-2082*

Jackson & Perkins
www.jacksonandperkins.com *800/292-4769*

Roses of Yesterday
www.rosesofyesterday.com *831/728-1901*

YARD AND GARDEN SUPPLIES

Charley's Greenhouse & Garden
www.charleysgreenhouse.com
800/322-4707

Duncraft
www.duncraft.com *888/879-5095*

Gardener's Supply Company
www.gardeners.com *888/833-1412*

Kinsman Company
www.kinsmangarden.com *800/733-4146*

INDEX

T

U-V

W-Z